Sunrise Prayers
with the
Family

SUSAN L. LONG

ISBN 979-8-89043-408-1 (paperback)
ISBN 979-8-89043-409-8 (digital)

Copyright © 2024 by Susan L. Long

All rights reserved. No part of this publication may be reproduced, distributed, or transmitted in any form or by any means, including photocopying, recording, or other electronic or mechanical methods without the prior written permission of the publisher. For permission requests, solicit the publisher via the address below.

Christian Faith Publishing
832 Park Avenue
Meadville, PA 16335
www.christianfaithpublishing.com

All biblical citations were taken from the King James Version (KJV), English Standard Version (ESV), New King James Version (NKJV), New International Version (NIV), and New Living Translation (NLT) of the Holy Bible.

Printed in the United States of America

Acknowledgment

All praise, glory, and honor be unto God the Father, God the Son, and God the Holy Spirit. Yes, the three are One, whom I believe has inspired me and given me the strength and an obedient heart to fulfill His will as it pertains to this book, Sunrise Prayers with the Family.

I dedicate this book to my mom, Mrs. Mamie Wiggins Smith, who transitioned to be with her Heavenly Father before this book was published. She was the one who prayed for me when I didn't even know Jesus Christ as my Savior and Lord. I remember a small black and white plaque from my childhood that my mom had on her wall that said, "A family that prays together stays together." These words always remained anchored in my heart even as I departed my mom's home to start my own family. The prayers in this book are actually prayers that I prayed over my spouse, children, and grandchildren. Thanks to modern technology, these prayers could easily be sent by text.

I also dedicate this book to my spouse, my children, and my grandchildren. Ervin L. Long, my husband for over thirty-seven years, who loves me without measure and has always encouraged me in the things of the kingdom of God. Ervin J. Long, my son who is full of compassion and love. It's his enthusiasm and energy that keeps me motivated. Eboni J. Long (Little Sue), my daughter who is full of love for others and always stands ready to lend a helping hand wherever she can. This young lady keeps me grounded and on the cutting edge.

A very special shout-out to my grandsugars—Patience A. Long, Decotah N. Long, and Cache CJ Long. May the angels of the Lord always surround and protect you.

Thanks, family, for believing in me. I love you all so very much. May God always get the glory from our lives.

In conclusion, the principle of praying at the set time and in the set place (1 Kings 18:18–39) taught to me by my pastors (R. Lee and Tina Tate) over the last twenty years has proven to be an invaluable spiritual asset in my life, so I give special thanks to them for providing spiritual leadership and insight to me.

Special acknowledgment to my brother, Robert L. Wiggins, and my church family, Montage at the Center of Worship in Converse, Texas.

Family Prayer

Father, we honor and bless Your name as we thank You for a new day, a new beginning in You. Thank You for a heart and mind to reach for You. So we come this morning intentionally praying for our family. We thank You that prayer draws us closer to You and it pushes back the kingdom of darkness.

Thank You for Your word in 2 Chronicles 7:14: "If my people, which are called by my name, shall humble themselves, and pray, and seek my face, and turn from their wicked ways; then will I hear from heaven, and will forgive their sin, and will heal their land."

Father, we humbly pray before You now. Thank You that we are a family that's committed to You and committed to prayer. We will not be divided. Our hearts are knitted together by the love of God. We lift each other up, encourage each other, and love each other as if we are loving our own bodies. We are a family that walks by faith and not by sight. We speak the Word of God with boldness, and we stand in great expectation that what we have spoken to our Father will come to pass.

We will not listen to the lies of the enemy; instead, we will turn our ears to listen to what is true and positive. We will prosper in the things of God. All our needs will be met. We will be the giver and not the borrower. We will share the good news of the gospel with all our Father sends our way, and we will be an extension of His hands. We say viruses and sickness will not come near our dwelling and we speak to what is there now, and we cast it to the pits of hell as we stand on Isaiah 53:5: "But He *was* wounded for our transgressions, *He was* bruised for our iniquities; The chastisement for our peace *was* upon Him, And by His stripes we are healed."

Father, we praise You now for a new beginning in You. We will intentionally come hard after You. In Jesus's name, we pray. Amen.

Rejoicing in the Lord

"This is the day which the Lord hath made; we will rejoice and be glad in it" (Psalm 110:24 KJV).

Father, with humble hearts, our family come before You this morning. We come magnifying You as our King. We come singing Your praises for allowing Your goodness and mercy to rest upon us. Thank You for the very breath flowing through our lungs. We also come pulling down every roadblock that the enemy has placed in our pathway.

We say we will walk victoriously in our Lord this day as we pick up our cross and follow Him. No weapon that is formed against us shall prosper. Every tongue that rises up against us shall be condemned. We now put on the whole armor of God, and we walk by faith and not by sight. We are strong in our Lord and the power of His might. We will hide the Word of God in our hearts, and we will open our mouths and speak it with boldness as our Father commands us.

We rejoice now because of the freedom our Father has given us. There's no more bondage in our minds or in our lives. We speak about those things that are not as if they are so. Our children rise up and call us blessed. We are givers to others of our time, talents, and treasures; and we love at all time. We are blessed by God and highly favored. Our God shall cover and keep us all the days of our lives. He will never leave or forsake us. No matter what, we will continually praise and worship His great name. In Jesus's name, we pray. Amen.

Family Prayer

"Let the heavens be glad, and the earth rejoice! Let the sea and everything in it shout his praise" (Psalm 96:11 NLT).

Father, we come as a family this morning shouting Your praises. You are indeed worthy of our highest praise. Thank You for keeping us throughout the night and allowing us to awaken to a new day in You. We confess our faults before You now, and we receive Your new mercies, which are new every morning. Great is Your faithfulness. The Holy Spirit teaches us to engage and abide in You. Let our focus remain on the things that our Father is calling us to do this day and remove the distractions and the pitfalls. We now move forward in our day, walking in the authority and power of Jesus Christ.

We "take therefore no thought for the morrow: for the morrow shall take thought for the things of itself. Sufficient unto the day is the evil thereof"(Matthew 6:34). We will run hard after our Lord, allowing Him to use all of us for His glory. Father, help us to wait on You in all things and not move ahead of You. Let our timing be Your timing in every situation that we encounter this day.

We say we are covered and protected by the blood of Jesus. We rejoice because we are His chosen ones, called, and appointed by Him. Father, speak on our behalf this day, saying, "And the Lord said unto Satan, The Lord rebuke thee, O Satan; even the Lord that hath chosen Jerusalem rebuke thee"(Zechariah 3:2). Thank You, Father, for all these things. In Jesus's name, we pray. Amen.

Family Prayer

Gracious and Eternal Father, we invite You to fill our rooms with Your presence as we make room for You. We come praying Your Word back to You. According to 2 Chronicles 7:14, "If my people, which are called by my name, shall humble themselves, and pray, and seek my face, and turn from their wicked ways; then will I hear from heaven, and will forgive their sin, and will heal their land."

We humble ourselves before You because our desire is to see You move on our behalf. Touch our hearts and give us a heart like Yours—hearts full of love and compassion, hearts that make room for You daily. We give the life that You have given us back unto You, praying that You use it for Your glory. Allow us to use the weapons that You have given us to pull down strongholds and put everything not like You under our feet. We say we are mighty and strong in You. We are healed and healthy, and we do not allow the cares of this world to overwhelm or overtake us. We will be steadfast in You, and the rain that falls in our lives and the wind that blows upon us shall not move us because we are standing on the solid rock, Jesus Christ.

As we go about this day, we will be aware of our surroundings, and we will not be overtaken by the enemy. We speak against every demonic spirit that has been assigned to us, and we say back to the pits of hell by the authority of Jesus Christ. Doors will be open in our lives that no one will be able to close. The promises that our Heavenly Father has made to us shall be fulfilled. We will live a life of freedom and not a life of bondage because all we need comes from the Lord. Thank You, Lord, for allowing Your grace and mercy to rest upon us. Help us to always set You as our number one priority in our lives. In Jesus's name, we pray. Amen.

The Father's Love Is Better than Life

"Because your love is better than life, my lips will glorify you. I will praise you as long as I live, and in your name I will lift up my hands" (Psalm 63:3–4).

Father, we come before You singing Your praises this morning, grateful that we are known by You and that You call us Your own. Allow Your grace and mercy to cover us as we ask now for forgiveness. We come now in the authority of Jesus Christ saying every weapon that is formed against us shall not prosper. They are cast down in our lives and back to the pits of hell. We are strong in the Lord and the power of His might.

We say what 1 Peter 2:9 says, "But ye are a chosen generation, a royal priesthood, an holy nation, a peculiar people; that ye should shew forth the praises of him who hath called you out of darkness into his marvellous light."

We hold onto Your Word, and we believe all that is written. We take back all that the enemy has stolen from us—our family values, our health, our treasures, our commitment, our peace, our love for others, our relationships with our family, our relationship with our Heaven Father, our pure and healthy mind, etc. Thank You, Lord, for restoring all back unto us.

This day and going forward, we will see through our Father's eyes, and we will speak what He speaks to us. Father, keep the negative thoughts and people away from our dwelling. Father, help us to think on Philippians 4:8:

> Finally, brethren, whatsoever things are true, whatsoever things are honest, whatsoever things are just, whatsoever things are pure, whatsoever things are lovely, whatsoever things are of

good report; if there be any virtue, and if there be any praise, think on these things.

Father, You are our all and all, so we ask You now to help us in every area of our lives. In Jesus's name, we pray. Amen.

I Will Exalt the Lord

"I will exalt you, my God the King; I will praise your name for ever and ever" (Psalm 145:1).

King of Glory, you are worthy, worthy, worthy, worthy. As a family, we will praise You, and we will exalt Your name. Thank You, Lord, for allowing Your mercies and grace to rest upon our lives once again. As we begin this day, we will "put on the whole armour of God, that ye may be able to stand against the wiles of the devil"(Ephesians 6:11).

We will intentionally listen to hear Your voice and obey all that You speak. Help each of us to look for opportunities to be a blessing to others. Let us walk with Your wisdom, knowledge, and understanding. If fear and doubt try to overtake our mines, we speak Your word to ourselves as written in 1 Corinthians 2:16: "For who hath known the mind of the Lord, that he may instruct him? But we have the mind of Christ."

Our family will be used mightily in these last days for Your kingdom business as You grant us an understanding that the lives we live are all for Your glory. We have tasted and seen that You are good, so help us to never turn to this world again in search of fulfillment and joy that only You can give.

Father, when things are not going the way we think they should be going in our lives, help us to walk by faith and not by sight and to hold on to Your hand and trust You like never before, knowing that You have the perfect plan for our lives. We thank You for hearing our prayer, and we believe You will move on our behalf, so we end this prayer with a kiss, giving You all of our hearts. In Jesus's name, we pray. Amen.

We Love You, God

"You shall love the Lord your God with all your heart and with all your soul and with all your might" (Deuteronomy 6:5 ESV).

Father, we come this morning with love and adoration for You our Lord and King, loving You with all that's within us, praying that Your Holy Spirit will come and help us to pray. We thank You for minds and hearts to draw near to You. James 4:8 (NKJV) says, "Draw near to God and He will draw near to you."

As we draw near, we confess our sins and ask for Your forgiveness. We invite You to come and have Your way with us as we begin again in You with clear hearts that only You can give. Grant us the required strength to walk on the pathway You have chosen for us as You grant us the required wisdom to take each step. Let us not be fearful when we can't see where the pathway is leading us. In these times, help us to trust Your hand to guide us.

Let us each be instruments of Your hands extending love to all. May we all be aware of our surroundings and not distracted by the sinful ways of this world. Teach us Your Word so we may live daily by it, as well as every word that comes from Your mouth. We will be a family that speaks Your Word with boldness, and we will wait to see it come to pass.

We say we have more than enough because our God supplies our every need. Give us ears to hear You clearly and let us not miss You as we go about this day. Keep back the hands of the enemy and help us to use the authority that You have given us against him. Let Your will be done in our lives. In Jesus's name, we pray. Amen.

Family Prayer

"I love you, Lord, my strength. The Lord is my rock, my fortress and my deliverer; my God is my rock, in whom I take refuge, my shield Or sovereign and the horn of my salvation" (Psalm 18:1–2).

Father, we come standing on Your Word this morning, saying You are our ROCK. As a matter of fact, You are our everything. We come as a family praying that You allow Your grace, mercy, and peace to rest upon us. As we start this day, let us start by worshiping and magnifying Your name. Forgive us for our sins and help us to live committed and dedicated lives unto You.

We will be people that love You with all of our hearts. We will intentionally seek Your face. We will give ourselves to You as a living sacrifice, to be an extension of Your hands and Your love. We rejoice now that we are known of You and that You hear us when we pray.

May our lips never cease to praise You. May our hearts always be full of love for You as You have shown Yourself strong on our behalf. May we never forget how REAL You are to us and may we daily come after You with a hunger and thirst that You only can quench. Keep us close to the cross and protect us from all evil and danger. Thank You for supplying all our needs. In Jesus's name, we pray. Amen.

Lord, You Are Our God

"Lord, you are my God; I will exalt you and praise your name, for in perfect faithfulness you have done wonderful things, things planned long ago" (Isaiah 25:1).

King of Glory, You have done it again. You awaken us with joy in our hearts and praise on our lips. So we come this morning, saying You are our God, You are the Lover of our soul, and You are the only One that has never done us wrong. We will boast in You because You have done marvelous things for us, and we don't think You are done yet. We come surrendering our will to Yours. We want the life that You promised us and not the one that we think is best.

Help us to walk victoriously with You, knowing we are chosen by the King. Let us leap for joy because of Your saving grace upon our lives. We will hold our heads up high because the Holy Ghost lives on the inside of us, and He gives us the power to fulfill Your will. Thank You that we are healthy and strong in the power of Your might. We are more than conquerors, and we have what we say because we speak what our Father speaks.

Father, help us to keep our focus on You and walk by faith and not by sight. Satan, the Lord rebuke you, get back to the pits of hell. You have NO authority over us, and we will not allow you to speak to us as if you do have authority over us. Father, continually surround us with Your presence, love, and peace. In Jesus's name, we pray. Amen.

Family Prayer

Good morning! Enjoy your day with Him.

Father, I honor and bless Your great name as I lift my family before You, praying that they remember You as they open their eyes this morning. Let praise and worship for You be their first words. Meet them where they are surrounding them with Your presence and love as they start their day. Help us to be a family that loves You with all our hearts, forsaking all to follow where You lead and giving up all to be committed and devoted to what You desire for us.

Clean our hands and purify our hearts so that we burn for You and only You. May our very lives be a living sacrifice for You. Let us hold nothing back from You but give You every part of us. Let us look like You, speak like You, and love like You. Help us to not be ashamed of this gospel, but let us share it boldly with all that You send our way.

Cover and keep us as You keep back the hands of the enemy. All assignments that he has for us, let them be canceled in the mighty name of Jesus. Uphold each of us with Your righteousness and let us intentionally seek You this day, not stopping until we have been apprehended by You. Stir up the gifts on the inside of us so they can be used for Your kingdom and not wasted.

Let Your Word come alive in us so we can walk by it and stand on it. Let us see ourselves the way that You see us, knowing we are fearfully and wonderfully made. We say You are our God and we are Your people—the ones that trust in You. In Jesus's name, we pray. Amen.

We Praise You, Lord

"He is the one you praise; he is your God, who performed for you those great and awesome wonders you saw with your own eyes" (Deuteronomy 10:21).

Father, I come with a heart of thanksgiving, grateful for Your hands resting upon me and my family as we go about this day. Let us magnify You and sing Your praises. May the Holy Spirit help us to stay engaged with You, to look for the move of God's hands upon our lives. Help us forget about yesterday and its troubles and let us press to be near our Father, accepting the mercies that have been granted this day. May we walk in the authority of Christ and be an extension of His hands.

May we never forget how much You love and care for us. Keep our minds at peace and let not the cares of this world overwhelm or overtake us. Allow Your presence to be with us wherever we go and let Your angels do warfare on her behalf.

Father, we stand on Your word this morning in 2 Corinthians 4:8–9 (NIV): "We are hard pressed on every side, but not crushed; perplexed but not in despair; persecuted but not abandoned; struck down, but not destroyed."

Thank You, Father, that You uphold us with Your righteous right hand. You are our Keeper and the One that protects us from all harm and danger. We say we are strong in You and the power of Your might. We will go forward this day, seeing ourselves the way that You see us—the chosen ones that have been called out to fulfill Your will on earth, the ones that are blessed above all measures, the ones that You delight in, and the ones that You desire to be with. Thank You for loving us just the way we are. Let us love You with all of our hearts. In Jesus's name, we pray. Amen.

Shout for Joy to the Lord

> Shout for joy to the LORD, all the earth. Worship the LORD with gladness; come before him with joyful songs. Know that the LORD is God. It is he who made us, and we are his; we are his people, the sheep of his pasture. Enter his gates with thanksgiving and his courts with praise; give thanks to him and praise his name. For the LORD is good and his love endures forever; his faithfulness continues through all generations. (Psalm 100:1–5)

Gracious and Eternal God, we come as a family this morning, singing Your praises, for it is You and You alone that have done marvelous things in our eyes. We come with hearts full of thanksgiving as we remember who You are to each of us—the I Am, that I AM—providing everything that we need. As we press into Your presence, we confess our sins before You, asking for Your mercies that are new every morning.

As we go about this day, let us walk hand in hand with You and listen so carefully to hear Your voice and obey all that You speak. As we draw near to You, our prayer is that You keep back all evil and danger. Let not the enemy come near our dwelling, and help us to fight the good fight of faith. We will pick up our cross and follow You, move by Your power and Your might, and cast down every roadblock that's before us. We are more than conquerors in Jesus Christ. Yes, Lord, it's in You that we move, live, and have our being.

No matter what we are faced with today, we will not quit, and we will put on the whole armor of God and continually march forward in the mighty name of Jesus. We come casting all our cares on

You because we know that You care for us, so we will not be moved by negative thoughts, negative conversations, or negative people. We will trust You to keep our minds stayed on You, keeping us in perfect peace. Thank You for hearing and answering our prayers. In Jesus's name, we pray. Amen.

Family Prayer

"Because he loves me," says the Lord, "I will rescue him; I will protect him, for he acknowledges my name. He will call on me, and I will answer him; I will be with him in trouble, I will deliver him and honor him. With long life I will satisfy him and show him my salvation." (Psalm 91:14–16)

King of Glory, You are mighty in all Your ways, so we come this morning, pouring out our love upon You, grateful for another day to sing Your praises. We come confessing our faults, asking for Your forgiveness as we go deeper into You this day. We set our hearts now to reach for You as we go about our day, seeking to know You and what is pleasing unto You. Let this life that we will live bring glory unto Your name.

We say now we will be faithful and dedicated to the call that's on our lives, and we will not quit when we don't see Your hands moving in our lives. But we will stand on the last words spoken unto us. We will not measure our lives or family by other people, and we will be grateful that we have a life and a family. We will pick up our cross and follow You, knowing the battle is not given to the strong but to the one that endured unto the end. We will continually draw our strength from You as we spend time at Your feet.

Open Your scriptures unto us so that we walk with understanding. Holy Spirit, come and be our Teacher and our Helper. We need You, and we welcome You into our lives. Father, grant us more of Your love, mercy, and grace so that we are all that You are calling us to be in these last days. Let Your healing oil rest upon us and heal our physical bodies, emotions, hearts, hurts, past, and minds. Let us be whole and complete in You. In Jesus's name, I pray. Amen.

Family Prayer

Father, I come this morning, lifting my family before You and praying that as we begin our day, we will begin it with praise and worship for You, remembering You as our Savior and Lord. Help us to forever trust You, according to Psalm 13:5–6: "But I trust in your unfailing love; my heart rejoices in your salvation. I will sing the Lord's praise, for he has been good to me."

Thank You for Your goodness toward us. May our life be one of dedication to You, forsaking all to follow hard after You, setting You as our first priority. Teach us how to love You with all of our hearts, to worship You in Spirit and in truth, and to remain committed to You. Teach us Your ways and help us not to depart from them. Keep us near the cross as we share the good news of the gospel with all. Help us not to fear when the gentle winds blow in our life, but remember that our lives are held in the palms of Your hands and You will keep us in the middle of any storm.

We say we will be faithful to follow You with all of our hearts, and we will remain focused on where You are leading us. Thank You that we have all that we need to fulfill Your will on this earth. We will want for nothing; all of our needs are taken care of by our Heavenly Father. In Jesus's name, we pray. Amen.

Family Prayer

"I love you, Lord, my strength. The Lord is my rock, my fortress and my deliverer; my God is my rock, in whom I take refuge, my shield and the horn of my salvation" (Psalm 18:1–2).

I come now lifting my family before You, praying that You allow Your grace and mercy to rest upon us as we start this day. Help us to set You as our first priority, bowing at Your feet to honor You as our God. Grant us hearts of worship to worship You as the only true and living God and to declare You are our Lord. Purify our minds and hearts and help us to put on the mind of Christ walk according to all that You speak unto us.

Let us love You with our whole heart being committed and dedicated to You. Help us to not let anything keep us from fulfilling Your will on earth. May we understand Your plan and purpose for our lives, knowing it's Your will that must be fulfilled. Keep back the enemy from our lives and keep us safe as we go about our day. We need You to keep us anchored to the cross, covered in Your blood. May we stop throughout our day to bless Your name. In Jesus's name, we pray. Amen.

Family Prayer

Glory to our King! Here we are as a family this morning, with arms wide open to You who loves me and has freed me from my sins by Your blood (Revelation 1:5). To You, be the glory and the dominion forever and ever (Revelation 1:6). We are grateful for the invitation to come and the reminder of Your great love. As we come with hearts of thanksgiving, we thank You for our very life and the privilege to be called Your own.

We are positioning ourselves to hear from You and receive bread from heaven. Speak, Lord. We are listening, and there's no other place we desire to be right now but at the cross, enjoying Your presence. Come, Holy Spirit, and allow us to engage with You. Forgive us for our sins and let us begin again this day. We say we are new in our Father and the sins of yesterday are behind us. We go forward this day, carrying our cross by the strength of our Father. We are the head and not the tail. Our enemy is under our feet. We are healed and healthy.

We speak the Word of God with boldness. We walk by faith and not by sight. We have what we say because we speak to what we hear our Father speaking. No weapon that is formed against us shall prosper because greater is He that's on the inside of us than he that's in the world. We are blessed when we come in, and we are blessed when we go out. We are the borrowers and not the lenders.

The presence of God surrounds us as we go about our day, and we can hear His voice clearly. We have hearts that obey all that our Father speaks to us. We set God as our first priority in our lives. We will be watchmen on the wall, standing in the gap for others. We confess and believe all that we have spoken will come to pass. In the mighty name of Jesus, we pray. Amen and amen.

Family Prayer

"To the only wise God our Saviour, be glory and majesty, dominion and power, both now and ever. Amen" (Jude 1:25).

Father, with a heart of thanksgiving, our family comes before You this morning, thanking You for Your faithfulness toward us. We come honoring You as our God, lifting our hands in praise, and opening our mouths with worship. This is the day You have made, and we will rejoice and be glad in it. Let our speech be uplifting toward all this day as we look for opportunities to be a blessing to all You send our way. We say we are chosen by You, and we will be used for Your glory. We will help those in need and show love and kindness to all even if they don't look like us.

We will give to the poor and share Your Word with boldness. We will be Your instruments to show others You are alive and that You still do miracles. We will not yield any parts of our bodies to be used by the enemy. We will surrender our all to our Lord so that we will be productive for the kingdom of God. We will not allow the cares of this life to distract us, but we will remember if you take care of the birds and flowers, surely, You will take care of us. So help us not to worry but to trust the moving of Your hands on our lives.

Thank You for meeting our every need and for helping us to walk upright before You. We say by Your stripes, we are healed, whole and complete—nothing lacking and nothing missing in our lives. Thank You, Lord, for Your word in 1 John 3:22: "And whatsoever we ask, we receive of him, because we keep his commandments, and do those things that are pleasing in his sight." In Jesus's name, we pray. Amen and amen.

Family Prayer

Heavenly Father, You are my refuge and strength—a very present help in trouble.

"Therefore I will not fear, though the earth be removed, and though the mountains be carried into the midst of the sea; Though the waters thereof roar and be troubled, though the mountains shake with the swelling thereof" (Psalm 46:1–3).

Whatever my lot, Thou hast taught me to say, it is well with my soul. Regardless of my season in life (Ecclesiastes 3:1–8), God, You have taught me to find internal peace in Jesus (Colossians 3:15).

So, Father, with Your Word on our lips, we come praying as we cast our cares upon You, knowing that You care for us! As we draw close this morning, let Your praise continually be upon our lips and worship for You in our hearts. Forgive us for our sins as we pick up our cross and follow You. Strengthen us for today's journey and help us to live today and not worry about tomorrow.

Supply our every need and grant us a heart to remain humble. Help us to love like You as we set You as our first priority. May we walk hand and hand with Your Holy Spirit as we remain engaged with Him throughout the day. Cover and keep us safe from the hands of the enemy. Keep our minds stayed on You so that we will have perfect peace.

Let us be joyful all day long as we think of Your goodness. Illuminate today's assignment for us so that we don't miss it. Our desire is to fulfill Your will and bring glory to Your name. Help us to love You with all our hearts. In Jesus's name, we pray. Amen.

Family Prayer

"I am crucified with Christ: nevertheless I live; yet not I, but Christ liveth in me: and the life which I now live in the flesh I live by the faith of the Son of God, who loved me, and gave himself for me" (Galatians 2:20).

Father, I come this morning lifting my family in prayer, thanking You for the very life You have given us. As we start this day, help us to renew our commitment unto You, open our mouths, and let us sing Your praises for Your love and kindness toward us. We have sinned against You, but we confess our faults and ask for Your forgiveness now. We say nothing will separate us from Your love. We step into this day by the power of God, walking boldly in His authority. We are not defeated. We are children of the Most High God, so we move into our rightful place as His heirs.

Come what may, we will look to our Father to help us overcome whatever we are faced with. We will fill our homes with the Word of God and live in the right now and not worry about tomorrow. We will intentionally make room for our God to dwell with us and rest upon us. We will set no evil before our eyes, and we will not allow our ears to be entertained by evil.

Our minds will stay on Christ so we will have perfect peace as we go about our day. We will have joyful hearts because our Father has made us glad. Teach us to love You more today than yesterday and to love our neighbors as ourselves. In Jesus's name, we pray. Amen.

Family Prayer

"Great is the Lord and most worthy of praise; his greatness no one can fathom" (Psalm 145:3).

Merciful King, glory be unto Your name! I come with a heart of gratitude, thanking You for Your love and kindness toward me and my family. We come with humble hearts, thanking You for watching over us throughout the night and allowing us to see this day. We pray that You would take all of us as we bow at Your feet, making room for Your presence. Holy Spirit, You are welcome here. Speak. We are listening.

We haven't always walked uprightly before You, but we ask for mercy as we begin again, setting You as our first priority. Saying this day, You are our Lord, and our desire is to please You with our lives. We are nothing without You, so come and take our hands and lead us throughout this day. Grant us ears to hear Your voice and hearts to obey. Help us to not think more highly of ourselves than we should, but let our thoughts be centered on You, pressing into Your presence to know You more.

Identify those that we should be a blessing unto and help us to love like You. We will put on the whole armor of God so that we can stand against the enemy. We will not back down, but we will trust in You to fight our battles. We say we are strong in You and the power of Your might. Our prayer is that You release complete healing over our family and let us testify of Your goodness. We love You Lord, and we will look for ways to put our love into action. In Jesus's name, we pray. Amen.

Family Prayer

"Let me give you a new command: Love one another. In the same way I loved you, you love one another. This is how everyone will recognize that you are my disciples—when they see the love you have for each other" (John 13:34–35).

Father, we come before You this morning with thoughts of how much You love and care for us, so we enter into Your gates with thanksgiving, praise, and worship, honoring You as our King! As a family, we bow at Your feet, inviting Your presence to fill the room. We make room for You because we want to be where You are and listen to the plans You have for us and love on You as our Savior.

What a love You have showered upon us, such joy and blessings You have given unto us. We give our very lives to You, praying You make something beautiful out of them. Grant us the required strength to walk according to Your plan and purpose for our lives and let us continually look unto You to be the Author and Finisher of our faith. No weapon that is formed against us shall prosper. We will walk victorious in our God. In Jesus's name, we pray. Amen.

Family Prayer

Father, I honor Your name as I come lifting my family before You, praying that Your hands rest upon them as they start their day in You. Let Your praise be upon their lips and worship in their hearts. Keep them safe as they travel today and let no evil come near their dwell. Keep the highways and the airways safe. Cover each in Your blood and keep the hands of the enemy far away. As they go forward this day, let each love You with all of their hearts as they bow in Your presence, loving You as their first love. Bless their going out and coming in and may Your blessings and peace overwhelm them as they cast all their cares at Your feet. Let each see themselves the way that You see them, fearfully and wonderfully made. Order their footsteps to fulfill Your will on earth. In Jesus's name, we pray. Amen.

Family Prayer

"God the only Lord—I praise you, God, because you are 'the LORD, and there is no other; apart from You there is no God'" (Isaiah 45:5).

Master, King of Glory, Lord of Righteousness, Savior, and Giver of Life, with a heart of gratitude, I bow at Your feet this morning, lifting my family before You, praying that they are overwhelmed by Your presence. Let them experience You in a way today like never before. Allow them to step into another level in You as they bow at Your feet, declaring You as their Lord.

Your word tells us in Matthew 6:34: "Take therefore no thought for the morrow: for the morrow shall take thought for the things of itself. Sufficient unto the day is the evil thereof." So we will be content with today as we cast all our cares at Your feet. We will not worry, and we will put all our trust in You.

Let us make room for You throughout this day and pause occasionally to worship and honor You. Help us to set no evil before our eyes and continually love You and others. Set a hedge of protection around Eboni as she travels today. Keep back the hands of the enemy and let her arrive safely. In Jesus's name, we pray. Amen.

Family Prayer

I praise you, God, because "who is like you, Lord God Almighty? You, Lord, are mighty, and your faithfulness surrounds you" (Psalm 89:8).

Father, I come this morning with a heart of thanksgiving, full of praise, and adoration for You. Thank You for remembering me and my family this day. My prayer is that You would allow Your grace and mercy to rest upon my family as I lift them before You. Let their feet be planted in You as they bow at Your feet. Let their hearts be encouraged as they remember how much You love them.

Grant them the required strength to meet every challenge that's set before them. Remove every hindrance that might try to block their journey, and send Your angels to safely lead them on the path that You have set before them. Allow men to give unto them and allow Your blessings to overtake them.

Keep back the hands of the enemy and let them lift their hands and magnify You as their King. Grant them healthy minds and bodies so they are able to fulfill Your will on earth. Let each hear Your voice and obey quickly. Let this be a great day for them as they see You high and lifted up. In Jesus's name, I pray. Amen.

Family Prayer

He giveth power to the faint; and to him that hath no might he increaseth strength. Even the youths shall faint and be weary, and the young men shall utterly fall: but they that wait for Jehovah shall renew their strength; they shall mount up with wings as eagles; they shall run, and not be weary; they shall walk, and not faint. (Isaiah 40:29–31 ASV)

Father, we come this morning to bless You as our King, lifting Your name on high because of who You are. Thank You for Your love and kindness toward me and my family as we start this day we start it in You, praising You with all that's within us. We will look unto the hills from which our help comes—You, the God who made the heaven and earth.

We will not be weary in doing well, but we will put all our trust in You and wait on You no matter what. Father, You know all our sins, but we come now confessing them and asking for Your forgiveness. Wash us and make us clean once again. We are so in love with You, so help us to openly display that love before You and others. Show us our assignments for this day, and grant us the required strength to fulfill them.

Thank You for the beautiful time we shared as a family over these past days, and may the memories last forever. And may we remember You were in the midst. Thank You for those that have already made it home safely and those that will make it home safely. We give You all thanks and glory. Watch over and keep us anchored to the cross as You cover us in Your blood. Help us to be a blessing to others this day. In Jesus's name, I pray. Amen.

Family Prayer

The LORD *is* my shepherd; I shall not want. He maketh me to lie down in green pastures: He leadeth me beside the still waters. He restoreth my soul: He leadeth me in the paths of righteousness for his name's sake. Yea, though I walk through the valley of the shadow of death, I will fear no evil: for thou *art* with me; Thy rod and thy staff they comfort me. Thou preparest a table before me in the presence of mine enemies: Thou anointest my head with oil; my cup runneth over. Surely goodness and mercy shall follow me all the days of my life: And I will dwell in the house of the LORD for ever. (Psalms 23)

Father, we come this morning, magnifying Your name and thanking You for Your love and kindness toward us. Our very souls shout hallelujah to the Great I Am that I Am! We will praise You, and we will exhort Your name because You have been so good to us. Thank You for opening our eyes to see You high and lifted up in our lives and for allowing Your mercy to rest on us.

We have life because of You and not just life but life more abundantly. We confess we are Your called-out ones that will move Your kingdom forward. We love with the love of Christ, and we are healthy, whole, and complete. We have the mind of Christ; the peace of God rest on our lives. We have perfect peace, and we walk by faith and not by sight. We are surrounded by angels, and they fight on our behalf. The enemy will not come near our dwelling; we always have more than enough. Our cups will always be overflowing because we live in the overflow.

We are faithful to our Heavenly Father, and we obey all that He speaks to us. When we sin, we will confess our sins quickly and return to the open arms of our Father. We love and trust Him, and we give ourselves completely to Him. Thank You, Father, for hearing and answering our prayers. In Jesus's name, we pray. Amen.

Family Prayer

"True worshipers will worship the Father in the Spirit and in truth" (John 4:23).

Our Father, we come this morning to worship You our King, thanking You for Your constant presence no matter where we are. With hearts of gratitude, we bow at Your feet, welcoming You to have Your way in our lives. We lay down our lives so You can live in us.

Help us to take no thoughts for tomorrow but to be content with this day, using every opportunity that's presented before us to bless and honor Your name. Help us to lock eyes with You this day to hear what's on Your mind and avail ourselves for Your use. We love You, and we lift our inner man before You, praying that You fill us once again with Your Holy Spirit.

Let us be a blessing to someone this day as we share Your love with all. We say we are healed, healthy, and blessed. All of our heart's desires are filled by our Heavenly Father according to His Will for our lives. In Jesus's name, we pray. Amen.

Family Prayer

Father, I come blessing Your name; I am so grateful for Your faithfulness toward me and my family! Your love is so amazing, and You are always nearer than we think. I come this morning, lifting my family before You, thanking You for allowing Your mercy and grace to rest upon us. I believe Your best for us is yet to come. We will continually put our trust in You.

Thank You for restoring every area in our lives—our relationship with You, our minds, our marriages, our family connections, our finances, our health, and our hope. Help us to live a committed life before You, forsaking all to follow where You are leading. Strengthen us to use our time wisely for Your glory. Help us love like You, and may we always set You as our first priority in our lives.

Blood of Jesus, cover us this day. Let our lives be profitable for the kingdom of God. May the wisdom, knowledge, and understanding of God rest upon us. In Jesus's name, we pray. Amen.

Family Prayer

"The Lord is my strength and my shield; my heart trusts in him, and he helps me. My heart leaps for joy, and with my song I praise him" (Psalm 28:7).

Father, thank You for putting a new song in our hearts, for allowing us to leap for joy this morning, and for knowing You are our everything. We come this morning as a family connected together with our hearts, praying that Your praises will be upon our lips, as we look to You to be our all and all.

Let Your peace rest upon us and let us not be troubled but trust You, knowing that You got us. Surround us with Your presence and let us feel Your love as we go about our day. Keep back evil, and use us for Your glory. Remove all worry and doubt from our minds and our hearts. Open our eyes to see all that You are doing in our lives. May we look to You to be the One that satisfies and sustain us.

Let us not trust in man or riches, but let us trust the plan You have for our lives. Help us to take the time to build a solid relationship with You and get to know You as our Father—the One that loves us and the One that has never done us wrong. Teach us to worship You in the Spirit and the truth and hold nothing back but continually reach for You. Thank You for moving now on behalf of Ja'mel, Alisha, and Eboni as it pertains to their new homes. May they not miss the move of Your hands and let them follow the leading of Your Spirit and standing on Your Word.

"Do not be anxious about anything, but in every situation, by prayer and petition, with thanksgiving, present your requests to God" (Philippians 4:6).

Thank You, Father, for moving on behalf of our family. In Jesus's name, we pray. Amen.

Family Prayer

Father, I come this morning with praise upon my lips, saying You are beautiful, marvelous in all Your ways, and full of grace, mercy, love, and kindness. I come lifting my family before You, thanking You first for being our God. As we start this day, let us start it with You by magnifying Your great name because You are so worthy.

Thank You for keeping us through the night and awakening us with a mind to reach for You. Help us to live this day so that our ways and our actions are pleasing unto You. Let us be the extension of Your hands and reach out to those You send our way and share Your love and obey all that You speak unto us. Help us not to waste time but to be focused on the Father's business and sacrifice our lives so You can live in us.

Let us not be entangled with this world's way of living, but help us to live victorious in You, abiding by all that You speak unto us. Our prayer is that You find something in us that You can use for Your glory.

Satan, the Lord rebuke you. You are under our feet as we walk this day, and no weapon that is formed against us shall prosper. We are healthy, and we walk by the authority of God. Come what may, we will not quit, but we will trust God's leadership in our lives. In Jesus's name, we pray. Amen.

Family Prayer

"One thing I ask from the Lord, this only do I seek: that I may dwell in the house of the Lord all the days of my life, to gaze on the beauty of the Lord and to seek him in his temple" (Psalm 27:4).

Father, we bless and honor Your name as we come before You as a family. Our prayer is that You cover and keep us as we begin this day. Let Your praises be upon our lips and Your Word in our hearts. Fill us once again with all of You. Help us to walk by faith and not by sight and let us lift You high in our lives. Let us set You as our first priority and make the time to set at Your feet and learn of You.

Show Yourself strong on our behalf and keep back the enemy. May You be our first desire and reach for You and wait for Your arrival. Let this life that we live bring glory unto Your name as we pray that Your will be done. Show us how to lean, trust, and depend on You to inquire of You before making life-changing decisions and to know that You stand ready to answer us concerning every part of our lives.

Help us to remember that everything that concerns us concerns You. Take us deeper into You this day as we press into Your presence. Keep our minds stayed on You so that we will have perfect peace. Welcome, Holy Spirit, come and lead us. In Jesus's name, we pray. Amen.

Family Prayer

"I praise you, God, because my salvation and my honor depend on you, oh God; you are my mighty rock, my refuge" (Psalm 62:7).

Gracious and Eternal God, You are strong and mighty, wonderful and excellent in all Your ways. We come as a family exalting Your name. Let our praises move Your heart to come a little closer to Your children that desire to meet with You. That's coming with hearts that are full of thanksgiving and that have taken the time to be with You, praying that You would pause to receive our sacrifice.

Let our offering be pleasing unto You as we bow at Your feet, praying You fill us up once again with all of You. We confess our sins and faults before You as we ask for Your forgiveness. Just as You were with Moses and You had a plan for him even as a child, we pray You be with us and reveal Your plan to us—where should we go, and what should we do and say once we get there?

Order our steps according to Your will, and grant us the required strength that's needed. Let us not worry at all, but help us to trust our very lives in Your hands. We will look to You for our provisions, and we will trust in Your power to do all that's required of us. We thank You for granting us Your peace that surpasses all understanding and giving us Your wisdom and understanding.

I lift Ja'mel and his family before You, praying You allow Your healing oil to rest upon them and drive out all sickness. Let them rise quickly from this sickness. Cover each of us as we go about our day and keep back the hands of the enemy. Let us remain focused on You and love You with all that's within us. Keep our eyes open for opportunities to be a blessing and to share the good news of the gospel. In Jesus's name, we pray. Amen.

Family Prayer

Father, as I come this morning, I lift my family before You, praying that You allow Your mercy and grace to rest upon them as they start their day. May they set their hearts and affections upon You as they remember You at the beginning of their day. Let them fall in love with You all over today and set You as their first priority, forsaking all to follow where You are leading. Order their footsteps and keep them on the path You have set them on.

Help them to keep their focus on You, knowing You are good and that Your leadership is perfect. Let them be the giver today as You use them as extensions of Your hands. Meet their every need as they trust You for everything. Let no evil come near their dwelling and let them hear You clearly. In Jesus's name, I pray. Amen.

Family Prayer

Our Father, which art in heaven, "Hallowed be thy Name. Thy Kingdom come. Thy will be done in earth, As it is in heaven. Give us this day our daily bread. And forgive us our trespasses, As we forgive them that trespass against us. And lead us not into temptation, But deliver us from evil. For thine is the kingdom, The power, and the glory, For ever and ever. Amen." (Matthew 6:9–13 KJV)

King of Glory, thanks be unto Your name. Thank You for Your Word, which we speak back unto You, as it flows from hearts of thanksgiving. Thank You for keeping us throughout the night and allowing us to be awakened by Your touch of true love.

As we come, we ask that You order our footsteps and place us on the pathway You have chosen for us. Help us to not get caught up in the who, what, when, and where but to just follow Your guidance. Season our words with salt so that they will be edifying and minister grace to the listener. Help us to rejoice in You throughout the day, knowing that You are near.

Let us not be frustrated and hard to get along with. Let us be pleasing in all our ways and have a desire for others to be in our presence. Show us how to show Your love to all that we meet. Help us to abide in You so You can abide in us. May we be the people that walk uprightly before You, loving You with all of our hearts, mind, soul, and strength.

Let us forget about yesterday and all its troubles and let us enjoy this day that's full of blessings. Let Your Holy Spirit dwell richly in us as we walk by faith on this King's highway, doing our part to fulfill Your will on earth. In Jesus's name, we pray. Amen.

Family Prayer

> Praise be to the God and Father of our Lord Jesus Christ! In his great mercy he has given us new birth into a living hope through the resurrection of Jesus Christ from the dead, and into an inheritance that can never perish, spoil or fade. (1 Peter 1:3–4)

Thank You, Father, for our inheritance—one that will never perish, spoil, or fade. I pray that my entire family is a part of this inheritance, and may they trust their lives to You and give up their lives so You can live in them. As we go about our day, may You be our first priority. May we allow You the required room and space to fulfill Your will and may our lives line up with Your will.

Teach us to love You with all of our hearts as we press into Your presence, desiring to know You more today than yesterday. Feed our inner man as we lift him unto You. We want to be strong in You and the power of Your might and defeat every enemy in Your name. Thank You that we are not forgotten and that we are chosen by You for Your good pleasure. Come, Father, and lead us throughout this day; and let us pause throughout the day to remember You and love on You. In Jesus's name, we pray. Amen.

Family Prayer

"Whatever you have learned or received or heard from me, or seen in me—put it into practice. And the God of peace will be with you" (Philippians 4:9 NIV).

Father, we come as a family, pressing into Your presence and desiring to meet with You to hear what You will say concerning Your will for this day. Thank You for allowing us to be a part of this day and for seeing something within us that You can use for Your glory. Thank you for loving us, being with us, and answering our prayers. You have been better to us than we have been to ourselves by watching over us, protecting us, meeting our every need, and blessing us over and over again.

Help us to never forget all our help comes from You—the God who made the heaven and earth. May we always remember You are with us, standing ready to perfect all that concerns us. Teach us how to love and how to be satisfied with just being with You, watching You move in our lives. Be glorified in and through us as we move at Your command. In Jesus's name, we pray. Amen.

Family Prayer

My son, keep my words and store up my commands within you. Keep my commands and you will live; guard my teachings as the apple of your eye. Bind them on your fingers; write them on the tablet of your heart. Say to wisdom, "You are my sister," and to insight, "You are my relative." (Proverbs 7:1–4)

Father, I thank You for Your Word as I come lifting my family before You, praying we will keep Your Word in our hearts and speak it out of our mouths and live by every word. Help us to look to You to be our everything, knowing all we need is found in You. Let Your Holy Spirit lead us as we go about this day, with our eyes open to see the move of Your Spirit.

Let us be centered on fulfilling Your will and not trying to do what pleases us. Help us to take the time to listen closely for Your voice, to inquire of You before making decisions that could change our lives forever. Breathe new life into us as we lift our inner man to You. Let us see the plans You have for us.

Keep back all evil and danger as we set our affections on things above and remember our lives are hidden in You. Allow Your mercy to rest upon us as we confess our sins before You. Teach us how to walk before You so that we can please You in all our ways. Let us love like You and let us help someone this day and share salvation as You lead us. In Jesus's name, we pray. Amen.

Family Prayer

"Teach me to do your will, for you are my God; may your good Spirit lead me on level ground" (Psalm 143:10 NIV).

Glory and honor be unto our King, the Faithful One, and the All-Knowing and All-Powerful in all His ways—the One that's full of mercy and grace and the One that extends love and kindness to all. Our prayer is that You would accept our invitation to come and be intimate with us to allow Your presence to fill the room as we bow at Your feet. With grateful hearts, we come before You. We are grateful that You have called us Your own, that You desire to dwell with us, and that You really do love and like us. As we come, ready our hearts and ears to hear Your voice and receive all that You speak unto us.

Let us understand what You are doing in this season of our lives and let us join in so that Your perfect will is fulfilled. Remove all doubts from our minds that tells us we are not worthy and that You have forgotten us—all lies from the enemy. We are chosen vessels, standing ready to be used by our Master. We rededicate our lives and reaffirm our commitment unto You. Take our lives and use them for Your glory.

Thank You for healthy bodies and minds, so we can continue on this journey called life. Help us to always trust in Your power and Your might, knowing we can do nothing but fail without You. Keep back the hands of the enemy and keep us safe in Your arms as we go about our day. In Jesus's name, we pray. Amen.

Family Prayer

Glory be unto the only true and living God, the One that gave His Son that we might live. As we come before You this morning, our prayer is that Your kingdom come and Your will be done on earth as it is in heaven. We confess our sins and faults before You and ask for Your forgiveness, and that as we go about this day, Your Holy Spirit would go before us and order our footsteps.

Jesus, we need You. We require You, and we want You. Please keep our minds stayed on You and our hearts turned toward You. We will look to You for our help. We pray that we hide Your Word within our hearts and let it be in our mouths as we speak.

Holy Spirit, we need Your power working in and through us, so come and be our help. Let us hear You and obey You. Let us be Your light in a dark world and lift You up so You can draw all men unto Yourself. We lift our inner man up before You.

Strengthen us to be strong in You and the power of Your might so that we don't quit. Fill us with Your joy—joy unspeakable—so that we don't worry about tomorrow. Be glorified in and through us, and show Yourself strong on our behalf as we completely surrender ourselves unto You. In Jesus's name, we pray. Amen.

Family Prayer

> Wherefore God also hath highly exalted him, and given him a name which is above every name: that at the name of Jesus every knee should bow, of things in heaven, and things in earth, and things under the earth; and that every tongue should confess that Jesus Christ is Lord, to the glory of God the Father. (Philippians 2:9–11)

Thank You, thank You, Lord, for another opportunity to just be with You, to exalt Your name and call You our own. Let the words of our mouth bless Your name as we honor You as our God. Let our coming be a pleasing sacrifice unto You.

As we come, we say we no longer want religion, but we want a relationship—an intimate love relationship with You—to know You like no other and to know Your thoughts and how to please You. Speak, Father, we are listening. We lay all our burdens at Your feet, and we pick up our cross to follow You. We no longer want to live this life according to what we think or feel; our desire is to allow Your Holy Spirit to direct our every footstep.

Let our thoughts and our ways be Yours. Take our lives and mold and shape them into Your good pleasure as we love You with all of our hearts. Thank You for keeping us on the journey You have placed us. Let us not look back into yesterday but look forward to all that You are doing in and through us for Your glory. Let us not worry but continually trust Your leadership in our lives because it is perfect. Thank You for Your word in Psalm 138:8: "The Lord will perfect *that which* concerns me; Your mercy, O Lord, *endures* forever; Do not forsake the works of Your hands." In Jesus's name, we pray. Amen.

Family Prayer

> The heavens declare the glory of God; the skies proclaim the work of his hands. Day after day they pour forth speech; night after night they reveal knowledge. They have no speech, they use no words; no sound is heard from them. Yet their voice goes out into all the earth, their words to the ends of the world. (Psalm 19:1–4)

Such an awesome God are You, full of tender mercies and compassion, loving Your children when we don't even think we deserve to be loved. As we bow at Your feet, help us to realize how much You truly love and care for us. Let us see through Your eyes that we can do nothing that would stop You from loving us, so take the burden from us, where we think we are not worthy, and release Your peace in our lives.

Remove the stress of the cares of this world from our lives and fill our lives with Your joy unspeakable so that we may enjoy every day You allow us to see. Open our eyes to see You moving in our lives and then let us realize we are blessed. We lift our inner man up before You, praying You fill us again so that we look like You, love like You, hear like You, and speak like You.

Let our one desire be to please You, making time to be with You and hear what's on Your mind and what thoughts You have pertaining to us. Guide our footsteps and lead us in the path of righteousness for Your name's sake. Help us to not quit, but to keep pressing onward in You. In Jesus's name, we pray. Amen.

Family Prayer

"One thing I ask from the Lord, this only do I seek: that I may dwell in the house of the Lord all the days of my life, to gaze on the beauty of the Lord and to seek him in his temple" (Psalm 27:4).

Yahweh, Yahweh, Yahweh, we come this morning, lifting Your name on high and praying Your Word back unto You. Come now as we invite You to fill the room with Your presence. Let us be a family that dwells in Your house all the days of our life.

Thank You for keeping us throughout the night as we start this day. Have mercy on us and go before us and prepare the way. Help us to follow where You are leading, and trust Your leadership in our lives. Help us to be an extension of Your hands and let us share Your love with all that You send our way. Let our desire be to please You as we take up our cross and follow You.

Keep us safe from all harm and evil as You cover us in Your blood. Let the joy on the inside of us overflow to others as we push past how we feel and what they look like. Use us for Your glory. In Jesus's name, we pray. Amen.

Family Prayer

Sing to the LORD, all the earth; proclaim his salvation day after day. Declare his glory among the nations, his marvelous deeds among all peoples. For great is the LORD and most worthy of praise; he is to be feared above all gods. For all the gods of the nations are idols, but the LORD made the heavens. Splendor and majesty are before him; strength and joy are in his dwelling place. Ascribe to the LORD, all you families of nations, ascribe to the LORD glory and strength. Ascribe to the LORD the glory due his name; bring an offering and come before him. Worship the LORD in the splendor of his holiness. Tremble before him, all the earth! The world is firmly established; it cannot be moved. Let the heavens rejoice, let the earth be glad; let them say among the nations, "The LORD reigns!" (1 Chronicles 16:23–31)

Father, we come this day with praise, worship, and adoration for You. Be highly exalted in our lives as we go about this day. Forgive us for our sins, and teach us Your ways as we abide in You and You abide in us. Thanks for remembering us on this day and allowing us to taste Your goodness. We give all of us unto You as we surrender our will unto Yours.

Let Your sweet peace rest on us and keep all evil away. We plead the blood of Jesus over our entire family. We shall not lack for anything. All our needs are supplied by our Heavenly Father. Our health is better than good, it's great. All blessings that are stored up for us is flowing down to us. In Jesus's name, we pray. Amen.

Family Prayer

> What shall we say, then? Shall we go on sinning so that grace may increase? By no means! We are those who have died to sin; how can we live in it any longer? Or don't you know that all of us who were baptized into Christ Jesus were baptized into his death? We were therefore buried with him through baptism into death in order that, just as Christ was raised from the dead through the glory of the Father, we too may live a new life. (Romans 6:1–4)

Father, I bless Your name as I lift my family before You, thanking You for our new lives—lives that are not our own but belong to You. As we begin our day, let us begin them honoring You, pausing to tell You how much we love You. Give us ears to hear You telling us our assignments for the day.

We pray that You Strengthen us to fulfill Your will on earth as we put all our trust in You, trusting we will walk in Your power and in Your authority. Forgive us for our sins as we move forward as Your chosen ones. Help us to abide in You and allow You to abide in us. Let Your love flow in our hearts and let us continually rejoice because we are Yours. Be glorified in our lives. In Jesus's name, we pray. Amen.

Family Prayer

Holy and Righteous Father, we come before You this morning with hearts of thanksgiving and with mouths full of praise. We say we love You and we desire to abide in You and have You abide in us. Thank You for remembering us, keeping us, and allowing us to see this day. We come giving our lives to You, praying that You make something beautiful out of them. Let them be used for Your glory as we go about this day.

Let us speak with faith and believe You will move mightily in our lives. Matthew 17:20 says, "Truly I tell you, if you have faith as small as a mustard seed, you can say to this mountain, 'Move from here to there,' and it will move. Nothing will be impossible for you."

We will stand on Your Word and say nothing is impossible for our God. Breathe new life into us, revive, and strengthen us for today's journey as we join in with what You are doing in this season. Let Your words be in our mouths as we speak, and let Your love flow from our lips. In Jesus's name, we pray. Amen.

Family Prayer

Heavenly Father, I come now with my family, thanking You for our very lives. Continually draw us close to You. Let us know that You love and care for us and that You have the perfect plan for our lives. Open our eyes to see Your goodness in the land of the living. Grant us the required strength to reach for You and seek Your face while You may be found.

Let us not put any other thing or person before You. May You always be our first priority. Overflow blessings upon us as we draw close to You and follow where You are leading. Let us love You with our whole heart and make time to be with You as we stay anchored to the cross.

Teach us all to wait on You for Isaiah 40:31 says, "But they that wait upon the Lord shall renew their strength; they shall mount up with wings as eagles; they shall run, and not be weary; and they shall walk, and not faint." In Jesus's name, we pray. Amen.

Family Prayer

I praise you, God, because "who is like you, LORD God Almighty? You, LORD, are mighty, and your faithfulness surrounds you" (Psalm 89:8).

Glory to our King! Thank You, Lord, for Your faithfulness toward our family. Thank You for drawing us near Your presence again with a mind to praise and worship You. We sing hallelujah to Your greatness because You are our God.

As we start our day, we confess our sins before You, praying You fill us again with all of You. We look to You now to order our footsteps in Your pathway of righteousness for Your name's sake. Help us to put all our trust in You and trust Your leadership in our lives. We believe You have called and selected us to fulfill Your will on earth, so we will look for the move of Your hands throughout this day and listen carefully to hear Your voice.

Set a guard over our mouths and help us to speak words that are edifying to the listener. Keep the enemy away and please cancel every assignment he has set for us. Cover us in Your blood and send Your angels to fight on our behalf. We believe there are more of them than us.

Breathe new life into us and strengthen us for today's journey. Help us not to quit as we lock hand and hand with You—the One that's by our side and the One that will never leave us. Surround us with Your peace and let Your joy be in our hearts. We love You, Father, and we pray You help us to put our love into action. In Jesus's name, we pray. Amen.

Family Prayer

The LORD reigns, let the nations tremble; he sits enthroned between the cherubim, let the earth shake. Great is the LORD in Zion; he is exalted over all the nations. Let them praise your great and awesome name—he is holy. The King is mighty, he loves justice—you have established equity; in Jacob you have done what is just and right. Exalt the LORD our God and worship at his footstool; he is holy. Moses and Aaron were among his priests, Samuel was among those who called on his name; they called on the LORD and he answered them. He spoke to them from the pillar of cloud; they kept his statutes and the decrees he gave them. LORD our God, you answered them; you were to Israel a forgiving God, though you punished their misdeeds. Exalt the LORD our God and worship at his holy mountain, for the LORD our God is holy. (Psalm 99:1–9)

Glory to God for He is our God, the One that has heard and still is answering our prayers. Father, we come this morning with mouths full of praise and adoration, grateful that You have remembered us another day and that You still have assignments for us on earth. Thank You that Your love never fails and that You are faithful. We empty ourselves of us, and we surrender to You, praying You fill us up with Your Holy Spirit so that we are led of Him as we go about our day.

Let us not be distracted by the cares of this life but remain focused on fulfilling Your will. Let Your love be seen in action in our lives as we reach out to others. Keep these bodies healthy so we are not hindered by sickness, disease, aches, pain and discomforts. We step out now in faith, saying by Your stripes we are healed.

    Carry us on the wings of Your love as You set a hedge of protection around us and all that pertains to us. Let us see where You are moving and what You are doing so we can join in as extensions of Your hands. We lift our neighbors up before You, praying that they can be drawn to You as we lift You up. In Jesus's name, we pray. Amen.

Family Prayer

To the One that speaks and light appears out of darkness, You are the One that made mankind in Your image and You are the One still holding the world in the palm of Your hand. You are the One we bow before, and You are the One we seek. You are the One we want to surround us with Your presence at this hour.

Father, as a family, we come praying that You would allow us once again to taste and see that You are good and to be partakers of Your overflow as we surrender our all unto You. We draw near with hearts of repentance, saying we have sinned and fallen short. Have mercy on us, Lord. Have mercy on us and let us begin again in You with clean hands and pure hearts, ready to fulfill Your will on earth.

As we go about our day, watch over and keep us. Let Your precious blood cover all of us. Open our ears to hear Your voice clearly and follow where You lead. May our desire be to be with You, to dwell in Your presence, and to love You with all of our hearts. Help us to set You as our first priority, forsaking all to follow hard after You.

May we all remember You have a plan and purpose for us and You are not finished using us just yet. May we rest in Your power and Your might, trusting in Your great name. Keep the enemy away and let him not come near, where he could try to kill, steal, and destroy us. We say, "Satan, the Lord rebuke you back to the pits of hell." In Jesus's name, we pray. Amen.

Family Prayer

Father, I bless Your name by saying You are worthy of all the praise and the honor—worthy, worthy, worthy. I bless Your name as I lift my family before You, thanking You for each of them. As they begin their day, let them begin it with You, seeking Your face, inquiring of You for Your plan for them. Help them to forsake all to follow hard after You. We will be a family that's committed to loving You with all of our hearts. We will stand ready to move as Your disciple to wherever You send us. We will open our mouths and speak Your Word boldly to all You send our way.

Fill us with Your Holy Spirit so we move by Your Spirit and Your might. Let Your peace rest upon us so that we are not overwhelmed with the cares of life. Allow Your presence to surround us as we walk by faith. Unite our hearts together as a family and let us love each other more than we love ourselves. Let us always see people through Your eyes and stand ready to be an extension of Your hands. Father, we belong to You, so come and have Your way. Not today, Satan. Go back to the pits of hell. We must be focused on our Father's business. In Jesus's name, I pray. Amen.

Family Prayer

"Sing unto the LORD; for he hath done excellent things: this is known in all the earth" (Isaiah 12:5).

Father, we come before You this morning, honoring You as our Lord—the Faithful One who has done great things in our lives and who loves us beyond measure. You have prepared a table before us in the presence of our enemies, and it's You who have kept us in the middle of the storm, bringing us through the fire without a mark on us. And how can we forget? It was You that healed our bodies over and over again. We say, "Hallelujah! Thank You, Jesus, for being our God."

As we start this day, we pray that Your mercy and grace rest upon us and help us to bring glory to Your name. We love You with all that's within us. Forgive us for our sins. Cover and keep us as You keep back the hands of the enemy throughout our day. Let us do our part to fulfill Your will on earth and spread Your love to all. In Jesus's name, we pray. Amen.

Family Prayer

Father, we honor and bless Your name as we lift Your name on high. Thanks for keeping us throughout the night and awakening us to a beautiful day! As we go about this day, order our footsteps and keep us in all Your ways. Keep us near the cross and let not evil dwell near us. Surround us with Your presence and protection. We will praise and exhort Your name as we make You known. We are in love with You, and You are our everything. Be glorified. In Jesus's name, we pray. Amen.

Family Prayer

Merciful God, thank You for remembering us this day and for allowing Your grace and mercy to cover our lives. With hearts of thanksgiving and reverence, we bow as a family before You. We invite You into our day. Come and overwhelm us with Your presence. Let our thoughts be consumed with You and let our hearts be wide open to all You desire to do in and through us. Help us to take the limits off of You as we give You free rein to shape and mold us for Your good pleasure.

Remove any and everything in our lives that's not pleasing unto You and replace it with Your will and Your desires. Let us love You with our whole hearts and grant You the space to be You in our lives. Teach us Your ways and help us live by all that is written, all that You have spoken, and all that You are speaking. We say we are more than conquerors in You. No weapon formed against us shall prosper because the Greater One lives in us. Help us to not be ashamed of the gospel and use each of us to reach someone for Your kingdom. Cover and keep us safe. In Jesus's name, we pray. Amen.

Family Prayer

Father, as we move even further into this Holy Week, we are so grateful for Your love that You would send Your Son to be the ultimate sacrifice for all mankind. What a love! Thank You, once again, for remembering this family and for keeping our minds stayed on You. With hearts bowed before You, we honor You as our Savior and our Lord! We invite You to come and walk with us today and share Your thoughts and plans with us as we yield all of us unto You.

Let the words of our mouths and the meditation of our hearts be pleasing and acceptable unto You. Order our footsteps in the pathway of righteousness and keep us humble before You. Let our desire be to be with You that You might send us forward for Your glory. Take all of us, for we are Yours, and we give all our love to You. Cover and keep us near the cross. In Jesus's name, we pray. Amen.

Family Prayer

"Whoever wants to be my disciple must deny themselves and take up their cross and follow me. For whoever wants to save their life will lose it, but whoever loses their life for me will find it" (Matthew 16:24–25).

Father, I come honoring You as my Lord as I lift my family before You, thanking You for giving us the heart to deny ourselves and taking up our cross to follow You. I pray You set each of us on fire for You, give us a fresh fire, and burn away everything that's not like You. As we go about our day, let our ways and actions be pleasing unto You. Grant us the required strength to fulfill Your will on earth.

Renew our minds and help us to put on the mind of Christ as we follow You with our whole hearts. Cover us in Your blood and keep back all harm, evil, sickness, disease, and danger. Keep us alert to what You are doing on earth and our in lives. Let us not miss the move of Your hands. We commit ourselves to be all of Yours and be glorified in and through us as we love You with all that's within us. In Jesus's name, we pray. Amen.

Family Prayer

"Saying, Father, if thou be willing, remove this cup from me: nevertheless not my will, but thine, be done" (Luke 22:42).

Father, I bless Your name as I lift my family before You, thanking You for keeping them and allowing them to see a new day in You. As they begin their day, let them remember You and how much You love them. Strengthen us to drink from the cup that's placed before us. Let their first desire be to honor You and love You with all of their hearts.

This is a good Good Friday—the day we remember the sacrifice of Your love. Set each one of them on fire for You once again as they bow at Your feet, seeking Your direction for their lives. May they set You as their first priority and press in to know You more today than yesterday. Cover them in Your blood and keep back the hands of the enemy from their dwelling. Help them to forsake all to follow You and please You in all their ways and actions. Teach them Your ways and to love like You. In Jesus's name, we pray. Amen.

Family Prayer

"Jesus Christ the same yesterday, and to day, and for ever" (Hebrews 13:8).

Father, how excellent is Your name in all the earth. You are the One that paid the ultimate sacrifice for us by laying down Your life that we might live. With hearts of gratitude, our family come before You this morning, letting You know we haven't forgotten You and Your precious blood. What a love.

As we start this day, we empty ourselves of our plans and our ways of doing things, and we submit our lives until You rearrange our schedules and order our day according to Your will and Your purpose. Keep us focused on You and touch those with love that You send our way.

Put smiles on our faces that will make others smile. Let Your words be in our mouths—words that will give others hope as we speak them. Be glorified in and through us and help us put You first and love You with all our hearts. In Jesus's name, we pray. Amen.

Family Prayer

Father, I honor and bless Your name as we come before You as a family, magnifying Your name and honoring You as our God. We confess our sins and faults, and we ask for Your forgiveness. We pray that Your mercy and grace cover us as we go about our day. Keep us surrounded by Your angels and allow them to fight our battles.

Let no evil come before our eyes and let it not enter our ears, hearts, or minds. Allow Your peace to rest on us. Help us to be examples of Your love as we recommit our lives to You. Burn away everything not like You and set us on fire for You. Strengthen our bodies to fulfill Your will. In Jesus's name, we pray. Amen.

Family Prayer

Father, glory be unto Your name! Our souls rejoice this morning for the new life You have given unto our family, so we cry out with loud voices saying we will praise You. We won't allow the stones to cry out for us. There's something on the inside of us that has to praise You. Hallelujah, hallelujah!

Come near this morning and consume our praise and worship as we come as a family, inviting You to have Your way with us. This life that You have given, we give it back to You, praying You use it this day for Your glory. Forgive us for our sins and faults as we go about our day.

Let us be reminded of who You are and let us intentionally do something to move Your heart. Teach us to be lovers of Your presence as You put Your desire on the inside of us to draw near to You. Keep us alert and help us to look for opportunities to bless You and others. In Jesus's name, we pray. Amen.

Family Prayer

"Sing unto the LORD; for he hath done excellent things: this is known in all the earth" (Isaiah 12:5 KJV).

Glory unto our God who has remembered us this day! Father, we come as a family, singing Your praises and making room for Your arrival. Come close to a family that desires to meet with You—a family that's hungry and thirsty for Your righteousness and a family that loves and adores You. We pour out our hearts before You, praying that You fill us with all of You and help us to be the disciples You are looking for to move Your kingdom forward.

Cleanse us from all unrighteousness and let us begin again full of Your Spirit and walk according to all that You are speaking unto us. Let our lives be pleasing unto You and available for Your use. Thank You for showing Yourself strong on our behalf and for opening doors that only You could open and closing doors in our lives that no man shall open.

You are the One that keeps on blessing us, making ways out of no ways, and breathing life on that which we thought was dead. We commit ourselves to You, praying that You will always be pleased to dwell with us. Keep us anchored to the cross and help us move at Your command and obey You with our whole hearts. Stir up our gifts and let them be used for Your glory as we love You and others. In Jesus's name, we pray. Amen and amen.

Family Prayer

> Praise ye the LORD. Praise God in his sanctuary: praise him in the firmament of his power. Praise him for his mighty acts: praise him according to his excellent greatness. Praise him with the sound of the trumpet: praise him with the psaltery and harp. Praise him with the timbrel and dance: praise him with stringed instruments and organs. Praise him upon the loud cymbals: praise him upon the high sounding cymbals. Let every thing that hath breath praise the LORD. Praise ye the LORD. (Psalm 150:1–6)

Hallelujah to the Great I AM! Father, we come this morning as a family to bless and honor Your name. You have been so good to us. Thank You that we have each other, but most of all, thank You that we have You—the Lover of our very souls. Let us never forget You and let us daily worship and praise Your name. As we go about this day, let us love all people—those who look like us and those who don't and those who do right by us and those who don't. Let us be Your true disciple.

We do like the apostle Paul today:

> Brethren, I do not count myself to have apprehended; but one thing I do, forgetting those things which are behind and reaching forward to those things which are ahead, I press toward the goal for the prize of the upward call of God in Christ Jesus. (Philippians 3:13–14 NKJV)

Cover and keep us all. In Jesus's name, we pray. Amen.

Family Prayer

> I give them eternal life, and they will never perish. No one can snatch them away from me, for my Father has given them to me, and he is more powerful than anyone else. No one can snatch them from the Father's hand. The Father and I are one.(John 10:28–30 NLT)

Father, we come as a family this morning, thanking You for giving us eternal life and for holding us safe and secure in the palms of Your hands. With hearts of gratitude, we bow before You, surrendering our will unto Yours, praying that You fill the room with Your presence. Speak to our minds and quiet our souls so that we can hear Your voice. We call on the name that's above all names: Jesus.

Jesus—there's just something about that name. Jesus, come into the room and turn over the tables of our lives and expose everything that's not like You. Father, remove the smallest things that are trying to spoil our vines of spiritual growth. We say we will not be moved from our steadfast place in You. Let the rains of Your mercy wash over us and make us pleasant to dwell with. Love of Jesus, spring up in our lives and give us an overflow of You.

Let us walk by faith and not by sight and let us trust You every step of the way. Give us, Holy Ghost, the boldness to share Your Word as we go about this day. As we continue on this day, let us be reminded that we are more than conquerors in Jesus Christ and that the Greater One lives on the inside of us. Satan, the Lord rebuke you, and we say you are defeated. Thank You, Father, for hearing and answering our prayers. In Jesus's name, we pray. Amen.

Family Prayer

> For God wanted them to know that the riches and glory of Christ are for you Gentiles, too. And this is the secret: Christ lives in you. This gives you assurance of sharing his glory. So we tell others about Christ, warning everyone and teaching everyone with all the wisdom God has given us. We want to present them to God, perfect in their relationship to Christ. (Colossians 1:27–28 NLT)

Our Father, come into this place and fill us once again with all of You as we make room for You. Forgive us for our sins as we confess them before You. Thank You for giving us the heart to believe Your Word and for opening our hearts and accepting You into our lives. Help us to stay committed to You by sharing Your Word, so others might be saved. Help us to maintain our relationship with You and to teach others to do the same.

May we look to You to supply all our needs and trust Your leadership in our lives. Cover us and keep back sickness, diseases, evil, and harm. Help us to remain faithful and to surrender unto You as we listen closely to hear and obey Your voice. In Jesus's name, we pray. Amen.

Keeping God's Name Holy

Father, may your name be kept holy. May your Kingdom come soon. May your will be done on earth, as it is in heaven. Give us today the food we need, and forgive us our sins, as we have forgiven those who sin against us. And don't let us yield to temptation, but rescue us from the evil one. (Matthew 6:9–13 NLT)

Father, we think You as a family for another opportunity to lift Your name on high and to adore You with our praises. Thank You for having mercy upon us throughout the night and allowing Your grace to rest on us this morning. We will never be able to thank You enough for all You have done for our family. Keep us focused as we go about this day and listen to hear Your voice and obey where You are leading.

Let not our hearts be troubled but let all our trust be in You—the One who made the heavens and earth. Help us to be a blessing to others by sharing Your love so freely with all You send our way. Let not the evil one come near our dwelling and let Your angels continually fight on our behalf. No weapon formed against this family shall prosper as we are walking by faith. In the mighty name of Jesus, we pray. Amen.

Singing God Praises

"But I will sing of your strength, in the morning I will sing of your love; for you are my fortress, my refuge in times of trouble" (Psalm 59:16).

Father, we come before You as a family, singing Your praises and worshipping Your great name, saying You are wonderful, beautiful, glorious, and matchless in every way. There's none that compares to You. We invite You to fill the room with Your presence and let our hearts be overwhelmed with You as we draw close to You.

We confess our faults, and we ask for Your forgiveness. We don't want anything to hinder Your arrival. With hearts of gratitude, we lift Your name on high, knowing that when we lift You up, You will draw all men unto Yourself. As You extend Your mercy and grace toward us this day, let us do the same for those You place in our pathway.

Let us love in actions and deeds and not just in words. You have been and are still being good to us, so help us to never forget all our help comes from You. Let not negative situations around us cause us to be negative but let us turn that negative into a positive for Your glory. Strengthen us to stand for what is right and pleasing in Your sight. Cover and keep us all the days of our lives and keep us anchored to the cross. In Jesus's name, we pray. Amen.

Lord Be Magnified

Unto the One who made the heaven and earth, be glorified, be magnified, and be exalted as we come as a family, lifting Your name on high! Thank You for breathing life into us this morning and for being the Keeper of our souls. We come thanking You for the hearts to draw near Your open fountain and allow Your blood to wash and cleanse us from all our unrighteousness.

We come freely, giving our lives unto You, inviting You to fill us with more of You. Grant us, Holy Ghost, the power to fulfill Your will on earth and for us to be mindful that the life that we live belongs to You. Open our eyes to the move of Your Spirit and help us to follow where He leads. We need You in our lives, and we require You in our lives. We cannot live these lives without You, so come and take complete control of every area of our lives.

Continually teach us Your Word and how to love like You. Let us be proof that You are with us and help us to be credible witnesses for You. Set a guard over our mouths today and help us to speak words that edify others and bring glory to Your name. Send Your healing oil to remove all sickness and disease from our lives so that we are capable of doing all that You require of us. In Jesus's name, we pray. Amen.

Family Prayer

Father, I bless and honor Your name as I come standing in the gap for my family. Thank You for keeping them throughout the night and allowing them to see another day. As they begin this day, let them start it with You by reminding them how much You love and care for them. May You be their first priority as they pause to remember You and recommit their lives to You. Allow Your peace, mercy, and grace to rest upon them as they reach for You.

Help them to know that Your ways are so much better, so may they trust Your leadership, knowing it's prefect. Open their eyes to see where You are moving and help them to follow You with their whole hearts. Let their every need be met as they trust You to be their source. Keep all evil away from their dwelling and cover them in Your blood. In Jesus's name, I pray. Amen

The Lord Is Our Rock

> To you, Lord, I call; you are my Rock, do not turn a deaf ear to me. For if you remain silent, I will be like those who go down to the pit. Hear my cry for mercy as I call to you for help, as I lift up my hands toward your Most Holy Place. (Psalm 28:1–2)

Father, I come lifting my family before You. Thanks for granting us a new day to honor and magnify Your name. As we go about this day, allow Your Holy Spirit to guide our footsteps and lead us in the path of righteousness for Your name's sake. We confess our sins before You; forgive us and allow us to begin again in You. Teach us Your ways, and help us to share Your Word with all as we set You as our main priority. Keep back the enemy and keep us close to You. May all we do and say be pleasing unto You and may we always trust You as our Source. In Jesus's name, I pray. Amen.

Family Prayer

Father, I honor Your name as I lift my family before You, thanking You for always being near when we call on You. So we come this morning, calling on You to surround us with Your presence and remove everything in our lives not pleasing unto You and grant us renewed minds and hearts that are on fire for You. Let us see ourselves the way that You see us—fearfully and wonderfully made.

Allow us to follow where Your Holy Spirit leads and help us to not be distracted by the cares of this life and rather put all our trust in You as we walk by faith and not by sight. Let us be a helper to someone this day by sharing Your love without reservation. Cover us in Your blood and keep back the enemy. In Jesus's name, I pray. Amen.

Jesus—the Name above Every Name

Jesus, Jesus, Your name is like oil poured out, filling the room. Jesus, Jesus, there's no other like You. Jesus, Jesus, You are wonderful, beautiful, glorious, and matchless in every way. As I come this morning, I lift my family before You, praying You have Your way with us. Have mercy upon us. Forgive us of all our sins and create clean hearts within us. Order Decotah's steps according to Your will.

Let us start this day anchored at the cross, looking to You to be the author and finisher of our faith. May we put all our trust in You, knowing Your leadership is prefect. Let us hear Your voice and follow where You are leading and forget the things of yesterday and look to see what and how You want to use us this day. Keep us and cover us in Your blood. In Jesus's name, we pray. Amen.

Family Prayer

Father, as I come this morning, I lift my family before You, praying You meet us just where we are bowed on our knees, worshiping You as the only true and living God. We open up to You now, saying You are welcome in this place. Come and dwell with us; come and have Your way with us. Breathe on us, fill us up with You, remove everything not like You, and direct our footsteps leading them to the plan and purpose You have for us. Teach us how to be fully committed to You and Your will and desire to please You with all that's within us. We give our all unto You so that we can be used for Your kingdom. Come and pour Your love upon us so we can love like You and be an extension of Your hands. In Jesus's name, we pray. Amen.

Special Prayer with the Family for Our Nation

"O Lord, thou art my God; I will exalt thee, I will praise thy name; for thou hast done wonderful things; thy counsels of old are faithfulness and truth" (Isaiah 25:1 KJV).

"The Lord is my strength and my shield; my heart trusted in him, and I am helped: therefore my heart greatly rejoiceth; and with my song will I praise him" (Psalm 28:7 KJV).

Father, with a heart of praise and thanksgiving, I enter the throne room at this hour, filled with gratitude that I am not forgotten and You still find pleasure in being with me. Words cannot express the feeling that I have—a feeling of completeness and wholeness, a joy that's unspeakable, a mind that's settled with Your peace, and a peace that the world did not give. So therefore, it can't be taken away by them. Your expression of love overwhelms me so until I am left speechless. The warmth of Your breath breathes new life into this broken vessel, allowing it to come alive once again. Yes, these dry bones will live again by Your grace and mercy.

Father, Your word tells us in 1 Timothy 2:1: "I exhort therefore, that, first of all, supplications, prayers, intercessions, and giving of thanks, be made for all men."

And 2 Chronicles 7:14 says, "If my people, which are called by my name, shall humble themselves, and pray, and seek my face, and turn from their wicked ways; then will I hear from heaven, and will forgive their sin, and will heal their land."

We come now with Your Word upon our lips, praying for our nation that violence and corruption would cease and men and women would return to their Creator with hearts of brokenness. Allow Your hands to rest upon our leaders, guiding them to make godly decisions that will lead us out of darkness and back into the light of Your glory. Breathe upon our economy and let it not crash, but let the market multiply so that the numbers are in the green for Your kingdom business and we become financially stable to move Your kingdom forward by leaps and bounds. In Jesus's name, we pray. Amen.

Family Prayer

Jesus—the Only true and living God, who's worthy of all the praise and honor—I come lifting my family before You, thanking You for Your love and kindness toward us. You have always been with us, and we are so grateful. As we begin this day, we begin by giving up control of our lives and saying we will not allow fear to control us any longer, but we will trust You to order our every footstep according to Your plan and purpose for our lives.

Wash our hearts and cleanse us so we are more like You. Renew our minds so that our thoughts are Your thoughts and our ways are Yours. Open our eyes to see like You, reaching those You send our way. Help us not to miss You. Illuminate our pathway so we are not hindered by any stumbling blocks.

Let us care more for others than ourselves. Release the treasures that You have for us so that they will be used for Your glory. We will look to You always to be the author and finisher of our faith. Yes, You are our source. Cover and keep us from all harm, evil, and danger as You keep the enemy from our dwelling. In Jesus's name, we pray. Amen.

Family Prayer

"To him who loves us and has freed us from our sins by his blood, and has made us to be a kingdom and priests to serve his God and Father—to him be glory and power for ever and ever! Amen" (Revelation 1:5–6).

I come, Father, lifting my family before You, thanking You for being our God and for allowing us another day to worship and honor Your name. As we come with hearts of brokenness, we pray You shake up the grounds of all our traditions and break down the walls of all our religion. Your way is better, so strengthen us to begin again in You walking according to Your will as we make room for You.

May You be glorified in our lives as we remember You this day. Let Your ways be our ways and let Your thoughts be our thoughts. Let us love like You and give ourselves up to the building of Your kingdom, forsaking all to follow You. Let Your blood cover us as You keep us from all evil and danger. In Jesus's name, we pray. Amen.

Lord, Our Trust Is in You

"Whoever dwells in the shelter of the Most High will rest in the shadow of the Almighty. I will say of the Lord, 'He is my refuge and my fortress, my God, in whom I trust'" (Psalm 91:1–2).

Father, I come this morning lifting my family before You, thanking You that Your love always remains the same. My prayer is that You allow Your mercy and grace to rest upon us as we begin this day. We have sinned against You, so we ask for forgiveness. Open our ears to hear Your voice, so we are obedient to all that You speak unto us. Draw us closer to You today than we were on yesterday, and let our hearts be fully engaged with You and give our all as we welcome You to abide in us.

Let Your love arise in us as we share it with all. Let us be surrounded with Your presence and help us to put our love in action toward You and others. Keep back the forces of darkness and release Your angels to fight on our behalf. We are more than conquerors in Jesus Christ, and we walk by faith and not by sight. Let Your praises remain upon our lips and worship in our hearts as we go about our day. In Jesus's name, we pray. Amen.

Family Prayer

"He is the one you praise; he is your God, who performed for you those great and awesome wonders you saw with your own eyes" (Deuteronomy 10:21).

Father, as I come, I lift my family before You, praying that You wash over us this morning. Rain down Your favor upon us, lavish Your love upon us, and pour out Your Spirit upon us. Allow us to taste Your mercy in the rain as we bow before You, honoring You as our Lord. Take all of us in exchange for all You. Take our lives and make them look like Jesus's. Let us love like You and be kind like You. As You have had mercy on us, let us show that same mercy to others.

Jesus, our hearts are open to You. You are the One we desire, the One that we seek, the One that we desire to please. Jesus, let Your name fill the room as we empty ourselves before You. Fill us so we are equipped to run the race that's set before us. Let us not quit but help us to depend totally on You to get us across the finish line with yet praise in our mouths.

The things the enemy has planned for us, stop it now in its tracks and let it move forward no more. Remove all roadblocks that are set up to hinder our pursuit of You, make ways out of no ways, and open doors that only You can open. Be glorified in our lives as we are focused on the Father's business. In Jesus's name, we pray. Amen

Family Prayer

Father, I honor and bless Your name as I lift my family before You. Thanks for allowing us to see another day, for giving us a heart and thirst to reach for You, and for seeking You while You may be found. As we start this day, breathe new life into us and fill us with Your Holy Spirit. Give us all we need to fulfill Your will on earth.

Let us stir up the gifts on the inside of us and use them for Your glory. When we speak, let Your words come out of our mouths; and when we love, let us love like You so others will see the proof that You are with us and we come in Your name. Keep back the hands of the enemy from our dwelling so we are not distracted by him. Be glorified in us. In Jesus's name, I pray. Amen.

The Lord Is Our Everything

"The Lord is my light and my salvation—whom shall I fear? The Lord is the stronghold of my life—of whom shall I be afraid" (Psalm 27:1 NIV)?

Father, I come standing in the gap for my family, magnifying and honoring You as our God. We open our hearts unto You, praying that You make them all new and give us hearts that are full of love and hungry for You and Your righteousness. Teach us how to totally submit our everything unto You and forsake all to follow You. Help us to not be ashamed of the gospel but to share it with all. Let us forever have hearts of thanksgiving and gratitude and remain humble as we walk before You.

Let our first love and desire always be unto You. Cover us with Your blood and help us to live blamelessly before You. Allow Your peace to rest upon us all as we chase hard after You and become a lover of Your presence. Thank You for blessing Alisha to see another birthday. Grant her and her heart's desire as she seeks Your will for her life. In Jesus's name, we pray. Amen.

Family Prayer

My son, keep my words and store up my commands within you. Keep my commands and you will live; guard my teachings as the apple of your eye. Bind them on your fingers; write them on the tablet of your heart. (Proverbs 7:1–3)

Father, I come lifting my family before You. Thanks for being our Lord. Help us to do all that You require of us as we begin this day. Help us to embrace You with all of our hearts, surrendering our will to Yours, so we can live victoriously in You. Forgive us for our sins. Guide our footsteps and lead us in Your pathway of righteousness as we forsake all to follow You. Come again and take over as we lift our inner man before You; fill us with all of You. In Jesus's name, I pray. Amen.

Family Prayer

"The Lord is my light and my salvation whom shall I fear? The Lord is the stronghold of my life of whom shall I be afraid" (Psalms 27:1)?

Father, I bless and honor Your name as we come lifting my family before You, thanking You for a family that's in love with You. As we start our day, let us start it by magnifying Your name and honoring You as our God. We will not lean upon our own understanding, and we will trust You in all our ways. We open our hearts unto You; come and fill us once again with all of You. Our desire is to please You, so open our eyes to see through Your eyes. Let our thoughts, behaviors, attitudes, and communication be that which is holy and acceptable in Your sight. In Jesus's name, I pray. Amen.

Family Prayer

"To him who loves us and has freed us from our sins by his blood, and has made us to be a kingdom and priests to serve his God and Father—to him be glory and power for ever and ever! Amen" (Revelation 1:6–7).

Father, I come lifting my family before You. Thanks for keeping us throughout the night and allowing us to see another day. Help us to lift our eyes to the hills from whence all our help comes—to the God who made the heaven and earth. Wash us and make us clean; take out everything in our lives that's not like You. Help us to be completely dedicated to You and fulfill Your will on earth. Strengthen us to work while it is day and love You with all our hearts. Strengthen us to not quit but to keep our eyes on You as we run the race that's set before us, trusting You to be the author and finisher of our faith. Let Your desires be our desires. In Jesus's name, we pray. Amen.

Family Prayer

Father, I come lifting my family before You, thanking You for our family and praying You continue to knit our hearts together as we give You first priority in our lives. As we start this day, let us start it by kneeling at Your feet, honoring You as our Savior and Lord. May nothing matter more than getting to You. Empty ourselves of our ways and thoughts, and let us surrender our will to Your will so we can do our part in fulfilling Your will on earth. Protect us from the forces of darkness and cover us with Your blood. Let our desire be to please You and reach for You with all of our hearts. Let us live for You and stand ready to be extensions of Your love to all those around us. In Jesus's name, I pray. Amen.

Hiding God's Word in Our Hearts

That he would grant you, according to the riches of his glory, to be strengthened with might by his Spirit in the inner man; That Christ may dwell in your hearts by faith; that ye, being rooted and grounded in love, May be able to comprehend with all saints what is the breadth, and length, and depth, and height; And to know the love of Christ, which passeth knowledge, that ye might be filled with all the fulness of God. Now unto him that is able to do exceeding abundantly above all that we ask or think, according to the power that worketh in us. (Ephesians 3:16–21)

Father, this is our prayer as a family this morning. Come and have Your way with us. In Jesus's name, we pray. Amen.

Family Prayer

"Finally be strong in the Lord and in his mighty power. Put on the full armor of God, so that you can take your stand against the devil's schemes" (Ephesians 6:10–11).

Father, I come standing in the gap for my family, thanking You that I have a family. As we start this day, let us put on the whole armor of God so we can stand this day, putting all our trust in You. Help us to look to You to be the author and finisher of our faith.

Cover and keep us as we go about our day and help us to keep praise on our lips and worship in our hearts. Let us love like You as we walk surrounded by Your presence. May we continually have a heart of gratitude for all You are doing in our lives. In Jesus's name, we pray. Amen.

Faith in God's Word

"Now faith is confidence in what we hope for and assurance about what we do not see" (Hebrew 11:1).

Father, I come now lifting my family before You, thanking You for Your faithfulness toward us and for keeping us throughout the night and awakening us this morning with a heart to reach for You. Father, when we didn't see how things would work out for us, we held on to our now faith and You moved on our behalf. Help us to be faithful in all our ways and to trust You when we can't see beyond our little ways of thinking.

As we walk with You, let us not doubt and let us not lean to our own understanding but help us to acknowledge You in all our ways, knowing You only want what's best for us. Cover and keep us and help us to keep our minds stayed on You and love You with all our hearts. In Jesus's name, I pray. Amen.

Family Prayer

"The Lord is my light and my salvation whom shall I fear? The Lord is the stronghold of my life of whom shall I be afraid" (Psalm 27:1)?

Father, I come this morning lifting my family before You, thanking You for our very lives and for being our light and our salvation. We will not be afraid of anyone because You are the Strong Tower of our lives. We rejoice because we are known of You. So as we start this day clothed with Your righteousness, pour Your Spirit into us and let us overflow with You. Use us to fulfill Your will on earth. Let us live for Your glory and Your good pleasure. Strengthen us to run the race that is set before us with patience and trust in You. Let us love You with all that's within us. In Jesus's name, I pray. Amen.

Family Prayer

"Great and marvelous are your deeds, Lord God Almighty. Just and true are your ways, King of the nations. Who will not fear you, Lord, and bring glory to your name? For you alone are holy" (Revelation 15:3–4).

Holy and righteous God, I come before You for my family, thanking You for being real to us and for allowing us to see another day and still have the heart to reach for You. As we come today, we hold nothing back. We will trust in You, the One who has always been faithful to us. Let Your worship and praise continually be on our lips and in our hearts as we reach for You with all that's within us.

We give our lives, so You can live in us, releasing our will for Yours. Help us to love like You, being so careful to move by the leading of Your Spirit. Let love continually knit our hearts together as we pray one for another and show each other that we care. Let us not think this life we live is about us, so help us to remember daily it's all about You. In Jesus's name, we pray. Amen.

Family Prayer

Grace and peace to you from God our Father and the Lord Jesus Christ, who gave himself for our sins to rescue us from the present evil age, according to the will of our God and Father, to whom be glory for ever and ever. Amen. (Galatians 1:3–5)

Lord, glory be unto Your name. Thank You for giving Yourself for our sins. I come this morning standing in the gap for my family, praying that we will love You with all our hearts and that we will never forget the grace that You have poured upon our lives. Forgive us for our sins and create clean hearts within us. How grateful we are that You allow Your glory to shine upon us.

Help us to see ourselves through Your eyes that we are fearfully and wonderfully made and loved by the Creator of heaven and earth. Strengthen us to be Your disciple and go throughout our day to make You known and lift You so You can draw all men to Yourself. Help us to forget about yesterday and any disappointments that came with it and let us press into Your presence and enjoy Your joy this day. Show Yourself strong on our behalf. Protect and keep us from all manner of evil and danger. In Jesus's name, we pray. Amen.

God's Ways Are Perfect

As for God, his way is perfect: The Lord's word is flawless; he shields all who take refuge in him. For who is God besides the Lord? And who is the Rock except our God? It is God who arms me with strength And keeps my way secure. (Psalm 18:30–32)

Father, I come this morning lifting my family before You, thanking You for our lives for giving us the desire to seek Your face and look to You to be our all and all. As we start this day, forgive us for our sins and cover us with Your righteousness. Strengthen us to run the race that's set before us, trusting You to guide our every step. May we be fully committed to You as we allow You to have full access to our lives. Cover and keep us as we love You with all of our hearts. In Jesus's name, we pray. Amen.

Family Prayer

"O give thanks unto the Lord; for he is good; for his mercy endureth for ever" (1 Chronicle 16:34).

Wonderful Father, we come before You this morning, singing Your praises, grateful for Your hands of mercy covering our lives. So we come as a family lifting Your name on high, bowing at Your feet, and honoring You as our God! As we go about this day, we pray that You send Your angels before us and that You surround us with Your presence. Keep our minds stayed on You so that we are at peace all day long.

Use us as an extension of Your hands to show love to those that are hurting and feel forgotten. Order our steps according to Your plan and grant us hearts to say it is well with our souls. Let us rejoice, knowing You have saved our souls and You are with us no matter what. We will praise You, and we will exhort Your name because You have been so good to us. Have Your way with us. In Jesus's name, we pray. Amen.

Family Prayer

Jesus replied, "Truly I tell you, if you have faith and do not doubt, not only can you do what was done to the fig tree, but also you can say to this mountain, 'Go, throw yourself into the sea,' and it will be done. If you believe, you will receive whatever you ask for in prayer." (Matthew 21:21–22)

Father, I honor Your name as I come lifting my family before You, thanking You for our lives. As we go about this day, let Your praises be on our lips and help us to not forgive the power and authority that You have given us. Help us to surrender our will to Yours so You can use us for Your glory. Surround us with Your presence as we pour out our love upon You. Cover and keep us, especially Eboni who is traveling. In Jesus's name, we pray. Amen.

Family Prayer

Our Father, I come now exhorting Your name—the name that's above every name. I come lifting my family before You, thanking You for blessing us with You. Grant us a heart and mind to continually seek Your face, forsake all to follow You, and make sure we give You first priority in our lives. Come and fill us once again with Your Spirit and strengthen us to fulfill Your will on earth. Let us love like You and become extensions of Your hands to reach others for Your kingdom. Help us to forget those things that are behind us and press into our today with You, living a victorious life in You. Help us to keep our minds on You, knowing You always have our best interest in mind. In Jesus's name, I pray. Amen.

Family Prayer

Trust in the Lord and do good; dwell in the land and enjoy safe pasture. Take delight in the Lord, and he will give you the desires of your heart. Commit your way to the Lord; trust in him and he will do this: He will make your righteous reward shine like the dawn, your vindication like the noonday sun. (Psalm 37:3–6)

Father, I bless Your name as I lift my family before You. Thanks for blessing us to see this day. May we always put our trust in You, committing our ways unto You and allowing You to order our every footstep. Cover and keep us and help us to keep our focus on You. Let us be satisfied with loving on You as our Father and enjoying Your presence surrounding us. Strengthen us for all that we will face this day and keep us steadfast in You.

Help us to not be shaken by the negative things going on around us. Let us be the ones that share Your love with all. Open our eyes to see You high and lifted up in our lives, fulfilling Your will on earth. Knit our hearts together as a family for us to love in actions and deeds and not just words only. In Jesus's name, we pray. Amen.

Let God's Will Be Done

> Therefore, I urge you, brothers and sisters, in view of God's mercy, to offer your bodies as a living sacrifice, holy and pleasing to God—this is your true and proper worship. Do not conform to the pattern of this world, but be transformed by the renewing of your mind. Then you will be able to test and approve what God's will is—his good, pleasing and perfect will. (Romans 12:1–2)

Father, I honor and bless Your name as I lift my family before You. Thank You for keeping us throughout the night. As we start this day, help us to give You first priority in our lives, presenting our bodies to You as living sacrifices. May all that we present be pleasing unto You. Order our footsteps and help us fulfill Your will on earth. Keep our focus on You as we go about our day, trusting You to surround us with Your presence and be very near when we cry out.

Show us things through Your eyes so we don't miss how You want to use us today. Let us love and comprehend like You and help our unbelief. Keep back the hands of the enemy so that we are not hindered from doing our part in seeing Your kingdom come and Your will be done on earth.

Strengthen our bodies where they are weak and heal those that may be sick. Help us not to quit but to maintain our testimony that our God is faithful and He will never leave or forsake us. Be glorified in and through us. In Jesus's name, we pray. Amen.

Family Prayer

"And I will give unto thee the keys of the kingdom of heaven: and whatsoever thou shalt bind on earth shall be bound in heaven: and whatsoever thou shalt loose on earth shall be loosed in heaven" (Matthew 16:19 KJV).

Father, we come as a family this morning, exhorting Your name and magnifying Your name because You have remembered us this day. There's none more worthy than You to receive all the honor and the glory. Let our lips never cease from praising Your great name. Let us daily be reminded that You are our God—the One who loves and cares for us, the One who has kept us, and the One who has given us authority in His name to bind and lose things on earth and in heaven.

Forgive us for our sins as we confess them and our faults before You. Help us to live a committed life before You, forsaking all to follow hard after You and allowing You to be our chief cornerstone—the sure foundation that we stand on when all other is sinking sand.

We will trust You, and we will follow You. We will love You with all of our hearts. Help us to not allow the cares of this life to pull us away from You. May we continually love You with all that's within us. Order our steps this day and let us love like You. In Jesus's name, we pray. Amen.

Family Prayer

Father, this is the day You have made; we will rejoice and be glad in it. Father, You are our good, good Father, whom we love so much. Thank You for giving us the heart to seek Your face, to want to be near where You are! We come this morning as a family, thanking You for giving us another opportunity to bless Your name.

Thank You for reuniting us together again. As we go about this day, keep us rooted and grounded in You. Help us to put all our trust in You and follow wherever You leading us. Let us not go ahead of You or get frustrated when we don't understand what You are doing in our lives. Keep back all harm and danger as we go on the highways and walk on Long's property.

Grant us supernatural strength to get their house in order so their lives can return to normal. Strengthen our love for one another and knit our hearts even closer together as a family. Help us to put on the mind of Christ as we go about this day and become extensions of Your hands and Your love. Help us to rest in You, following You with our whole hearts. In Jesus's name, we pray. Amen.

God's Love

> For God so loved the world that he gave his one and only Son, that whoever believes in him shall not perish but have eternal life. For God did not send his Son into the world to condemn the world, but to save the world through him. Whoever believes in him is not condemned, but whoever does not believe stands condemned already because they have not believed in the name of God's one and only Son. (John 3:16–18 NIV)

Thank You, Father, for coming after us. So this morning, we come after You as a family, thanking You for Your tender mercies toward us this day. All that we have, we bring it unto You, praying You can make something beautiful out of it for Your glory. We confess our sins before You now, praying that You create a clean heart within us and renew a right spirit in us as we draw close to where You are, lifting Your name on high.

Help us to always make room for You. Uphold us with Your righteous right hand and deliver us from our enemies. Set a guard over our mouths as You keep our hearts and minds pure before You. Let Your love flow from us to others and help us to be a blessing to others. Let not the enemy come near our dwelling and keep death away. Strengthen us to fulfill Your will on earth as we keep our minds stayed on You.

We say we are strong in You and the power of Your might. We are more than conquerors in You, and we walk by Your power and Your authority. We have more than enough. Our cups will overflow with You, and we will boldly share the good news of the gospel. Order our steps as we give You complete control of our lives. In Jesus's name, we pray. Amen and amen.

Family Praying Together for Family Member's Birthday

Father, this is the day You have made, and I will rejoice and be glad in it. I come lifting my family before You, thanking You for our very lives—lives that are dedicated to please and walk by the leading of Your Spirit and lives that are committed to fulfilling Your will on earth. Thank You for allowing our family member to see another birthday. Let him know You more this year than last year, and set a guard around him and let him hear Your voice clearly.

Fill us once again with Your Spirit by strengthening us to do all that You require of us this day. Help us to forsake all and come after You with all of our hearts, doing our part to make You known on earth. Teach us Your ways and let us live by every word that comes from Your mouth. Burn away everything in our lives not like You.

Help us to totally depend on You and obey Your every word. Let us not quit the race that's set before us but trust You to help us finish victoriously in You. Come and be the center of our lives. Open our eyes to see where You are leading so we *do not* miss You. In Jesus's name, we pray. Amen.

Lord, Our Hearts Pant for You

"As the deer pants for streams of water, so my soul pants for you, my God. My soul thirsts for God, for the living God" (Psalm 42:1–2).

Father. I honor You as I come standing in the gap for my family, thanking You for our very life and for allowing us to see this day. Our very souls are thirsty for You; fill us up Lord, fill us up at this hour. We lift Your name on high as we seek Your face, crying out for the true and living God. Fill us once again with all of You.

Our souls long for You to be near Your presence and to hear what's on Your mind. Strengthen our inner man as we surrender our will to Your will. Let this day be filled with You and draw us near to where You are, humbling ourselves before You, listening as You order our every footstep, and following where You are leading. We will stand on Christ, the solid rock, while all other is sinking sand. We will put all our trust in our Creator because He cares for us.

We will look at this life through His eyes, trusting He has the perfect plan for us, even when we don't understand it all. Satan, the Lord rebuke you. You have no authority in our lives. We are faithful sons and daughters of the Most High God—the One who we are committed to follow with all our hearts. Come, Father, and be glorified in us. In Jesus's name, we pray. Amen.

Family Prayer

Therefore, my dear friends, as you have always obeyed—not only in my presence, but now much more in my absence—continue to work out your salvation with fear and trembling, for it is God who works in you to will and to act in order to fulfill his good purpose. (Philippians 2:12–13)

Father, I come lifting my family before You, thanking You for giving us life this day. Let the life that You have given us be used for Your glory as You order our footsteps. Fill us with Your Spirit and help us to be fully committed and dedicated to fulfilling Your will on earth. Help us to set You as our first priority, listening so carefully to hear and obey Your voice. Keep back all evil and help us love like You. Remove any and everything in our lives that's not like You. In Jesus's name, we pray. Amen

Sing Joyfully to the Lord

Sing joyfully to the Lord, you righteous; it is fitting for the upright to praise him. Praise the Lord with the harp; make music to him on the ten-stringed lyre. Sing to him a new song; play skillfully, and shout for joy. For the word of the Lord is right and true; he is faithful in all he does. (Psalm 33:1–4)

Father, I come standing in the gap for my family this morning, saying our victory is in the name of Jesus. So we come lifting Your name on high, inviting You to come in and have Your way with us. Let Your praise continually be upon our lips as we go about this day. Use us to be a blessing to others and let us love You with all that's within us. Order our steps and set a guard over our mouths. Let not our speech betray us. Keep our minds stayed on You and keep us with perfect peace. Let not the enemy come near our dwelling. In Jesus's name, we pray. Amen

Family Prayer

"Lord, the God of our ancestors, are you not the God who is in heaven? You rule over all the kingdoms of the nations. Power and might are in your hand, and no one can withstand you" (2 Chronicles 20:6).

Father, I come honoring You as my Savior and my Lord as I lift my family before You, thanking You for remembering us this day and for granting us a heart to reach for You. We ask for Your forgiveness as we lay down our plans and invite You to take control of our surrendered lives. Order our footsteps and lead us beside the still waters and through the valleys. Let Your will be done as we cast all our cares upon You.

Let us feel Your presence standing by our sides as we live this life for You. Remove the blinders from our eyes so we see ourselves and our lives through Your eyes. Help us to always set You as our first priority. Teach us Your Word and let us live by it and every word that comes from Your mouth. Take complete control of our lives and help us to take no thoughts for tomorrow, trusting in You with our all and all. In Jesus's name, we pray. Amen.

Family Prayer

Glory be unto the faithful God our Father, the One who loves without measures. Father, with hearts of thanksgiving, we bow at Your feet at this hour, honoring You as the only true and living God! We make room for You to come and fill us again with Your Spirit. Our desire is to be molded and shaped into the disciples that You desire us to be on this day. Open our eyes to the urgency of these last days, and put us into position to receive Your Spirit as You pour it out upon the earth.

Grant us wisdom and knowledge to win souls for Your kingdom and to point man unto the One who loves without measures. Strengthen us to stay in the race that's set before us and not quit, looking to You daily to supply all that we need to keep running hard after You.

Purify our hearts and our minds and help us to be holy as You are holy. Keep us away from that which is corrupt and help us to be totally dependent upon You. Let us embrace Your presence all day long as we make You known. In Jesus's name, we pray. Amen.

Family Prayer

Glory be unto the only true and living God, the One who is above all—holy and righteous in all His ways. Father, we come as a family, thanking You for remembering us this morning, granting us hearts of thanksgiving as we reach for You, and seeking You while You may be found. Let our coming be an acceptable sacrifice unto You and may it move Your heart to draw near to us.

Forgive us for our mistakes, for trying to live this life on our own terms, and for taking pleasure in our sins. We repent now, turning back to You with our whole hearts. Help us to walk according to all that You speak unto us as we lean and depend on You. We are not perfect, but there's no doubt that we are in love with You. We give ourselves over to Your will and purpose for our lives, desiring to lift You on high so You can draw all men unto Yourself.

Teach us to live a lifestyle of holiness—a life that You will be pleased to come and dwell there on the regular. Let us be a living testimony that the presence of God walks with us. Breathe a new life into us as we lay at Your feet, waiting to hear all that You will speak. We will take up our cross and follow You, not worrying about tomorrow, knowing You are holding us in the palms of Your hands safe from all evil and danger.

Come and be glorified in and through us as we listen carefully to hear Your every command. In Jesus's name, we pray. Amen.

Family Prayer

> And I heard every creature in heaven and on earth and under the earth and in the sea, and all that is in them, saying, "To him who sits on the throne and to the Lamb be blessing and honor and glory and might forever and ever!" (Revelation 5:13 ESV)

Father, You are so worthy of all the praise, honor, and glory. There is no other God like You. You are awesome in Your ways, so we come with hearts of thanksgiving, inviting You to come and take complete control of our lives, as we give our will over to Your will. Let this life that we live be committed and dedicated to You. Let our ways and thoughts be pleasing unto You, where You will desire to dwell with us, that You will find pleasure in our presence.

Teach us to be loving and caring so others will see Your love in and through us. Keep us healthy so we are not hindered from doing the things that are set before us. Most of all, keep us in love with You, setting You as our first priority. In Jesus's name, we pray. Amen.

Family Prayer

To the only wise God, glory be unto Your name—the name that's above every name, the name that kings bow before, and the name that every knee will bow and confess His majesty. We come this morning, making room for You, saying our desire is to be in Your presence. So come close and wash us as we confess our faults before You. Allow Your new mercies to fall upon our lives and strengthen us to recommit our lives unto You.

As we go about this day, show us how to take the limits off and see You in every corner of our day. Renew our minds so that we think like You. Purify *our* thoughts so that they are pleasing unto You and let our actions bring glory to Your name. Send Your angels before us and allow grace to follow us as we set our affection on things on high. We will walk by faith and not by sight, casting our cares on the One who cares for us. In Jesus's name, we pray. Amen.

Family Prayer

Father, You are wonderful in all Your ways. So we come this morning as a family to love You, to bring You an offering of thanksgiving, and to make room for You to do whatever You want to do in our lives. You have been so faithful to us, allowing us to enjoy a relationship with You and to have hearts that reach for You and minds that take pleasure in being with You. We don't take it lightly that we get to experience the realness of who You are and that You have allowed us to taste and see that You are good.

Keep us rooted and grounded in You and locked into the things that really matter—the things that have eternal value. Let us daily check our holy investments and make sure our heavenly returns are greater than our earthly returns. Fill us once again with Your Spirit, equipping us to run the race that's set before us, stopping as needed to cry out for Your mercy and grace.

Help us to love like You and not to waste time with the small foxes that come to spoil the vine. Help us to trust Your leadership in our lives as we rejoice in You, our King. In Jesus's name, we pray. Amen.

Family Prayer

To the only wise God—who has all power in His hands and is full of goodness and mercy, who loves without measures—come and have Your way as we lift You this morning. Allow Your train to fill the courts of our hearts as we bow at Your throne. You are welcome to move in any way You desire to get us in the ready position and to stand against anything that might come our way.

Strengthen us to fight the good fight of faith, leaning and depending on Your leadership. Just as You ordered David's footsteps, order ours and let us hear You clearly in every situation, seeing everything and everyone through Your eyes. We say a special prayer of healing for Cache. Remove everything from his body that's making him sick and let him be healed quickly, if there's any way possible. Keep this sickness away from the other family members.

Keep our hearts on fire for You and keep the enemy far away from our pathway. Grant us our heart's desire as we remain steadfast in You, doing our part to be Your disciples. Grant us traveling mercies. In Jesus's name, we pray. Amen.

Family Prayer

Worthy is the Lamb of God. Father, You are holy and righteous in all Your ways. There's none that compares to Your greatness. With hearts of thanksgiving, we bow at Your feet, honoring You as the great I AM. Thank You for remembering us, allowing us an opportunity to reach for You, and giving us hearts that desire You. We give our lives unto You for Your kingdom business. Use all of us to bring glory to Your name and fulfill Your will on earth.

Open our eyes to see our assignments this day and help us to successfully complete them. Come and fill us with Your Spirit so that we are moving in Your power and Your might. Take complete control of every area of our lives and let us be Your true sons and daughters of the gospel—the ones who will forsake all to follow You. Strengthen our inner man to withstand whatever will come our way and help us not to quit, totally depending on You in all things. In Jesus's name, we pray. Amen.

Family Prayer

Heavenly Father, I come magnifying Your name as I lift my family before You. Thank You for Your tender mercies toward us and for allowing us another opportunity to reach for You. Fill us once again with Your Spirit as we empty ourselves of ourselves. Cover us with Your blood as You encamp Your angels around us, keeping back sickness and disease, violence and destruction, evil and chaos, and depression and doubt.

Let this life that we live bring glory unto Your name as we witness for You this day. Teach us to love all people and be a helper to those in need. Let us walk by faith and not by sight, trusting each of our steps is ordered by You and directed according to Your plan and purpose for Your will to be fulfilled on earth.

Keep us close to the cross as we worship and adore You. We ask that You allow Your healing oil to cover our grands, especially Patience. Let her ears be completely healed quickly and she can continue to enjoy her summer. In Jesus's name, we pray. Amen.

Family Prayer

"As I learn your righteous regulations, I will thank you by living as I should" (Psalm 119:7 NLT)!

Gracious and eternal Father, glory be unto Your name. This is the day You have blessed us; we will rejoice and be glad in it! We invite You to come and rest, rule, and abide in our hearts as we submit our will unto Yours. Let our lips echo Your praises as we go about this day, making room for You to be glorified in and through us.

Strengthen us to take up our cross and follow You, trusting the best is yet to come in our lives as we lean and depend on Your leadership. We lay our lives down, making room for You to do whatever You want to do. Fill us with Your Holy Spirit so that we are excellent witnesses for Your kingdom, lifting You so You can draw all men unto Yourself.

Overflow our hearts with Your love so that we are known as children of the Most High God. Keep back the hands of the enemy and let us walk in peace, health, and safety this day. In Jesus's name, we pray. Amen.

About the Author

Susan L. Long is a servant and friend of the Lord, who is dedicated to having an intimate relationship with Him. She believes this relationship is cultivated by a lifestyle of daily seeking Him, allowing herself to be apprehended by Him, and apprehending Him in worship, praise, and prayer. It's the quality time in His presence that she believes matures the relationship. Her heart's desire is to know God more day by day and to be known by Him.

Printed in the USA
CPSIA information can be obtained
at www.ICGtesting.com
LVHW040042251124
797341LV00003B/535